UNDERGROUND MANUAL FOR MINISTERS' WIVES

UNDERGROUND MANUAL FOR MINISTERS' WIVES

Ruth Truman

Abingdon
Nashville

Library of Congress Cataloging in Publication Data

TRUMAN, RUTH, 1931-
   Underground manual for ministers' wives.
   1. Clergymen's wives I. Title.
   BV4395.T7   253'.2   73-23060

ISBN 0-687-42796-7

MANUFACTURED BY THE PARTHENON PRESS AT
NASHVILLE, TENNESSEE, UNITED STATES OF AMERICA

Dear Bonnie, . . .

Fore! Word

The hand at the small of my back was insistent. The voice matched.

"Go ahead, dear. I want you to meet every one of the ladies!"

Before me were over a hundred loyal members of the local WCTU, come to our church for their annual Christmas party. None was younger than my mother, and some older than my grandmother. My feet felt glued to the floor. The hand pushed with more determination . . .

And so it went, time after time after time. I met them all, and a thousand more like them . . . and some of them became wonderful people in my life. Some weren't so wonderful, but I learned a lot from them about what not to be and how not to act!

You see, I had dragged my feet from the beginning. As a girl growing up in a Methodist parsonage I had vowed I would never, no *never*, marry a minister. A favorite boyfriend became an ex-boyfriend when he announced his intention to enter the ministry. So when I met this exciting young man who was headed for the mission field I knew I was safe. Little did I dream that a seminary professor would change his direction or that a bishop would discourage him from entering the foreign mission field because he needed pastoral ministers

in his conference. It happened though, and there I was—
a reluctant minister's wife who distrusted church people,
was determined to have privacy for her family, and
equally determined to do all the right things so her
husband could succeed. After all, I was pledged to be
his wife no matter what he chose to do with his life,
and his wife I would be even if it killed me—which it
almost did. Six years after our first appointment I lay
in a hospital bed recovering from surgery and rediscover-
ing life and people.

Emptiness and bitterness had become my companions.
There was no sense of self left. I had lived my life at the
whim of children and church, and the real me was almost
dead—but I got a second chance. I learned a lot about
me, about other people, about life and death, joy and
sorrow. And I discovered that many of my friends who
were ministers' wives were also in trouble because no
one had prepared them to live as full persons regardless
of their husband's job.

That is where this book begins . . .

Ruth Truman

Contents

1. The True You   **11**

2. In Sickness and in Stealth   **25**

3. The Happy Hour   **39**

4. The Insufferable Little Children   **51**

5. Love Thy Neighbor   **65**

6. Parsonage Roulette   **81**

7. Everybody Shift   **94**

8. The Hostess with the Leastest   **105**

9. The Love of Money Is Sin   **121**

10. Meditate! Meditate! Meditate!   **139**

11. The Original Eve   **149**

12. Let this Cup Pass from Me   **161**

The Last Word   **175**

1
The True You

Let's get one thing straight right from the start. The ministry is not just a pro-fession. It is more like an ob-session.

And you, unpaid, unsung focal point of your minister's life (provided said minister is your husband!) may feel like a pos-session.

That nine-minute wedding ceremony did it. One minute you were anonymous and carefree—then presto, bingo!—you are somebody you never met before. You have two new titles. One comes before your name and the other comes after it: Mrs. ————, the minister's wife. The first title puts your head in the clouds and finds you doing all sorts of odd and interesting things— cooking meals, running a home, signing your checks wrong, sleeping with a man . . . And every bit of it is for real, complete with society's Gold Seal of Approval.

It's hard to get used to this new person you suddenly are. You don't feel as though you belong in the old married set, but your single friends' lives become more separate from yours every day. Some of them seem to think you are actually a different person from the girl they knew just a week or two ago. Is it just because you're married? You keep getting this funny feeling that it is the other title people keep tacking on to the end of your name that makes them think you've changed. For sure, this title keeps your feet on the ground.

The seminary told you that people don't think of the minister's wife as special or unique anymore, except in some small segments of the country. The seminary goofed again! Of course, they don't put us (I'm one too!) in crates when we travel the way they did in the early days, nor are we told what to wear (most of the time!) or what we should do in the church (except by a few people). The stigma on our children has eased, so that they play with the parishioners' kids like any other pagan-born. Naturally they risk contamination that way and increase the possibility of criticism when they act like everybody else, but for the most part life is pretty normal for you and them. Different, but approaching normal.

Yet the idea is disturbing: is it because you are married to a man who happens to be a minister that people are treating you differently—or does this happen to every new wife? That must be it. You are exaggerating your feelings, and, given some time, they'll go away. Take all the time you want—five, ten, fifteen years. The new-bride complex is bound to wear off sooner or later.

Long before the first five years are up you will begin to realize that what is normal for anybody else may not be normal for you. There is a whole list of things people still frown at. Remember the first time you lost your temper and used a mild invective? You were as surprised as the lady who spilled her tea, but not for the same reason. You really didn't expect her reaction, did you? Or how about the time they called on you to pray when you were laughing hilariously, and try as you would you never did get through the prayer? The reaction at the swim party over your bikini was a little wild. Some of those women haven't recovered yet! Things are definitely different. People *do* seem to have other expectations of you than you have of yourself.

People seem to enjoy pointing you out, too. At first you wonder if you are suffering from paranoia, what with heads turning when you come into church, or women gesturing in your direction while whispering to their friends. Sometimes it is more obvious, like the usher who tries to direct you to "the minister's wife's pew" (second from the front directly in line with the pulpit). If you take this on as a challenge by sitting in a different place every Sunday, you may sink in your seat just in time to overhear the woman in front of you whisper to her husband, "I just never know where the minister's wife is going to sit anymore!" Or slide in late to a meeting, and the chairman is sure to say that she is *so* glad to see that "our minister's wife" has arrived. Definitely not the treatment other people get . . .

If you're not careful, you will begin to think you are supposed to be perfect. At housekeeping, child-rearing, entertaining, church work, spiritual living—wife exemplar! Of course, *you* know that you are clumsy; you always say the wrong thing at the right time; you've scarcely learned to pray in private, let alone in public; you buy all drip-dry clothes because you can't iron a thing without scorching it; and you've just begun to figure out your husband. When he preached on the text "take up your cross and follow me," you didn't figure he was speaking to you personally! You run over the marriage vows in your mind with relief—you didn't pledge to be perfect. "For better or worse" surely implied that you get a chance to learn what to do when and how. The question is, Where to start?

Since you're head over heels in love with your husband, let's begin with him. Why on earth did you marry him anyway? I know; he was different. When I first laid eyes on my husband, he was dashing up a flight of stairs three at a time, wearing a camel hair coat that looked as though it had been slept in (it had), levis, and engineer's boots. I thought, "Wow! That's really different!" and was immediately interested since I had never dated a fellow who didn't wear slacks and sport shirts. Imagine my surprise when I discovered that he also raced cars, flew planes, loved to soar, skied every time the snow fell, painted oil canvases, created art objects with a torch, could quote historical data like an encyclopedia, had his ham radio license, was majoring in experimental psychology, was an expert mechanic and photographer, could quote the Bible in great segments from memory, and was in love with me! He was really different—*vive la différence!*

In short, he had a zest for life, a love for people, and a deep humility before God. I've known hundreds of ministers in my forty years, and have come to the conclusion that those who really thrive on the ministry have these three qualities. In other ways natural to him, your man probably does too, and these are the very things that caught your attention—and may soon cause you tension.

Such a man is not easily encased in a box called a house. He just has to live in the whole world. Add to this the fact that he may feel God has specifically set him on a mission in life, and you may begin to feel that you rank somewhere around fourth or fifth in his hierarchy of people. (Careful, such a thought could lead to a martyr complex and have a fiery conclusion.) It's much safer to face the fact that God, not you, has first claim on your husband's life. And since he's a minister, would you want it any other way? How your lover expresses that claim can give you a little trouble, though. For example, he may be one of the fifteen-hour-a-day variety, for whom work is all-consuming. This man would probably work twenty-four hours if he could, just to make sure he packed everything possible into life *and* he would do it *whether or not* he was in the ministry. Work is his life, and he is happiest when he's accomplishing something. Other than for making him the way he is, God is rarely responsible for such a phenomenon. Neither is the church, though it may encourage him to work constantly. If this is your man, you just have to accept it: it's the nature of the guy.

I can almost hear the screams of protest rising from desert town and mountain village that the church makes the demands that keep a man working for hours after other men have ceased. True there is always lots to do, but your man is his own boss. He has to account to himself and God (O.K., and the church officers) for the way he spends his time, and how well he organizes it. He can do as little or as much as he wants to, within reasonable realms of satisfying his congregation. That isn't the issue. The question is—are you willing to let him be free to answer to himself and God in the manner he feels is best?

Now, of course, if you wonder where he is every time he goes out the door, if you suspect every afternoon call to hold the possibility of a sexual liaison, or if you need to know all the details of everything he has done during the day just so you can be sure he has been working the way he says he has, then you will not let him be free because you don't trust him. (Which implies that you don't trust yourself either!) I am fully aware there are ladies-in-waiting in every congregation, but 99 percent of them are waiting for somebody else, and your husband isn't what they had in mind. The issue is still there—you have to trust your husband, and he has to trust you, probably more than in any other profession. Such trust is very healthy for a marriage, incidentally . . .

Fast on the heels of freedom and trust comes the need to share him endlessly. When I was a little girl, I used to get very aggravated because somebody would always die just when our family planned to go somewhere. This feeling stayed with me well into the early years of our marriage, and even though my head told me that people didn't deliberately get sick or have trouble just as we were leaving on that long-awaited vacation, my emotions would still get tangled up with the little girl inside me who just wanted to climb in the car and drive away. It took awhile, but it finally dawned on me that the finest thing I had to share with other people was my husband, and when I could do little, because of family or other responsibilities, at least I could share him. Gift wrapped, yet!

People are the reason your husband is in the ministry (unless, God forbid, *you* are the one who wanted to be a minister and have pushed him into it!). You happen to rank as people, too, and it is much easier to give freedom, trust, and sharing if you both know where the work ends and the family begins. Attitude is the key. If you are great to be with, if you are a source of love and joy, he will try much harder to make free time for you. My husband firmly believes that the secret of John

16

Wesley's success was that he was so unhappily married it was a pleasure to stay away from home.

But why talk about your husband at all since this chapter is supposed to be about you? Good question. Actually, this is a roundabout way of talking about you. The questions are all yours to answer: who do you think has first claim on him? Are you willing to share him endlessly? Do you trust him? These are questions that shape your attitude toward the life-style you find yourself in, and the answers form the base of strength for your marriage. They require of you a self-examination that yields dividends in inner awareness. Your answers may not agree with mine, but ask the questions. That's the important thing!

That done, let's take a look at you through other people. Do you have some predetermined idea of what they expect of you? Maybe you've read a book that tells you to dress in navy blue, wear your hair conservatively, carry your Bible like a growth, and *never, never* look sexy. I threw a book like that clear across the room once! No other book has inspired me so much—to put on the sexiest dress I own (which really isn't very) and go out with my husband in his clergy collar. (Anyone knows that a priest is not supposed to have a dame hanging on to his arm—especially if he's married to her!) This book has no intention of telling you how to dress, but for your own mental health you need to examine and separate what you do because you want to from the things you do because you think you're supposed to. People outside have a neat word for this condition of life. It's called "hypocrisy." The New Testament expressly forbids it. But how we ignore that injunction! We buy our car, dress ourself and our kids, keep up our lawn all based on what the neighbors—or somebody—will think. If wire frames for glasses are in, we get wire frames. Clothes hang unworn in the closet because they are out of style. Granted, it's the American Way, and you learned it at your kindergarten teacher's knee when she insisted that you sit in the circle just like everybody else at story time. Result? Confirmed conformers.

Only now there is a slight twist. You may be expected to pray but not wear boots and mini-skirts, while your parishioners do just the opposite. But twist again, because the expectation may be only in *your* mind, not in theirs. Since you think they would criticize you for acting in a certain way, you don't do it, and then they come to expect you to act in the way you have been acting. You brought it on by not being true to yourself in the first place!

Some knowledge of your motivations is needed, however, to know what is true. If your attitude is "I'll show them," you will probably succeed—in appearing foolish and alienating your congregation. Or if you're out to embarrass your husband into leaving the ministry, this is certainly one way to do it. (You may have to use a few other tactics as well, but this attitude is a handy tool.) *Some* place along the line you have to decide that how you act, what you say, where you go, and what you wear are all self-determined. You can decide to do what you think "they" want, or to do what you want, but in either case the choice is yours so don't blame the church or some imaginary critic if you don't like the person you are showing to the world. It's *your* expectations for you that count, not theirs . . .

Now, if that last statement is true (and I declare it so!), you have a new task—that of finding what your goals for yourself really are. What standard of behavior do you have for you? What do you want out of your marriage? What is your life purpose? Why not boggle your husband by presenting him with a list of hopes and expectations some night. Not only will he understand you better, but he might even be joggled enough to do some self-searching of his own!

While you're taking a look at your hopes, you might assess your talents and skills. I know one minister's wife who went through twenty years of feeling inferior because she had never gone to college! She also happened to be one of the most skilled needleworkers I have ever met and could cook circles around me (and I majored in home economics in college). When God handed out the talents, he didn't give them to us equally . . . or did he? Maybe the problem is that some of us refuse to recognize that what we have to offer is just as valuable and necessary to society as the talents others have. Granted, some talents are seen more readily. If you sing, you have to stand in front of people, and it is easy to see that you have talent—or don't, as the case may be. It is fairly rare to stand on the stage and perfect a piece of needlepoint to the overwhelming applause of an audience. But I ask you, what would the singer give if she also had the time (which, because of practice, she doesn't) to adorn her home with handiwork? God gave you your gifts to use, so at least be proud of your Resource material.

A few words ago we were talking about giving your husband away—sharing him, to be exact. How willing are you to give your talents and abilities away? If ever a woman has an opportunity to use everything she is capable of doing, it is as the wife of a pastor. To share

19

your self freely is an art, sometimes only learned by observing the masters—or the Master. It is necessary, however, to be discriminating. Many are the people who have cringed through the struggled renditions of a hymn knowing that at least one person there could play it better but had not been asked because the minister's wife volunteered so easily. When you're good, be good; but when you're bad—take lessons!

Since I mentioned the woman who was bothered about her education, how do you feel about yours? Keeping alert to the world of knowledge is a real ego-booster. It helps you make conversation more easily. You feel more at home when ideas are discussed (and there will be a lifetime of them!) and you can share thoughts with your husband on a more equal level. Any kind of interest that keeps you thinking is valuable; any learning you acquire will increase your understanding of the world you live in and the people you share it with. Certainly, there is no excuse today for a woman to feel inadequate because of her education when it can be so easily corrected with TV courses, correspondence schools, public adult education, and university extension courses.

All this talk about you may make you feel as though you are being very self-centered. Glad you mentioned it. How self-centered are you? If your thinking theme-song is "Me, Me, Me," how do you possibly expect to enjoy others? In fact, you can expect to be downright miserable in the parsonage if you are the only person you think about. People will be banging their fists trying to get into your self, while you are busy barring the door from the inside. The louder they bang, the thicker the barricade you'll build until you finally discover that you have locked up your self so securely that even you have for-

20

gotten how to get out. If this is where you are, you need professional help to show you how to open the door again to interpersonal relationships. It was my opportunity to go through a wall-shattering encounter-group experience, for which I shall be forever grateful. My life turned the night a group member flung out the challenge: "Why don't you come out from behind that minister's wife role and start being a real person?" From such a crushing beginning has come a very full life.

Before the full, abundant life came, there had to be time to get acquainted with me, to ask some of the questions in this chapter, and ultimately to find out who I was. The answer was to come in three parts.

First, I had to discover that being my husband's wife was not my whole person, but that I had allowed it to become that. The church hadn't done it, nor had my husband; I had—by not daring to be me, by not saying the things I felt, by not being the natural person who was inside me. I had to learn to trust my intellect, to discover that only I must accept me. That one was hard. Finally, it hit me that God had made me the way I was and how could I dare reject his product? I even had to recognize the fact that I would never be the kind of minister's wife my mother had been—nor could I be, because I wasn't my mother. Can you imagine? I had to discover that I had a face people would remember, and therefore I could talk to people more easily. (I had always waited for the other person to speak first, just in case he didn't know who I was.) In short, my hang-up was to separate my inner life from the intelligent man I loved long enough to discover that I had some brains, too. How dumb!

That left me with freedom to explore the amazing fact that I had a life to live and was equally and separately responsible for that life. That certainly puts a new light on things. If you goof, you don't just take the blame; you have to figure out what you did that made things turn out wrong and then not do it the same way next time. Life suddenly becomes a challenge instead of an endurance race. A startling discovery was the fact that the more I was me, the better people liked me—the old snob image dropped away as it should have because all it consisted of was fear—of people, of new experiences, of myself.

And then I had to rediscover myself as a child of God. With this discovery the Self that had been prepared could blossom and life could turn on a completely new keel that could withstand the difficult and let me rejoice in the blessings.

Granted, your hang-ups won't be mine, but they might come close. Finding inner security is a pretty common human need not confined to the parsonage. In fact, it has very little to do with your husband's work, but everything to do with how you feel about the life-style you live as you react to his work and the people you come in contact with every day. It affects your marriage relationship, the way you live with your children, the ease with which you meet new people and re-meet acquaintances. To wit, when the inside person feels confident, the outside world looks great! Whether you're married to a doctor, a lawyer, or an Indian chief . . .

When you ask the question "Who am I?" you may need to ask yourself how you spend your time, your money, and your thought life in order to find the an-

22

swer. If large chunks of any of these three things are spent on you, out of proportion to other members of the family, you have developed a first-class clue. For example, it's a good idea to look as good as you can, but if every spare minute is concentrated on hair, face, wardrobe, and figure, it would appear that you are trying to convince someone (probably you!) that you are an acceptable person. The trouble is, you are starting in the wrong place. Acceptability comes from the inside out, not the outside in.

In searching for goals, you could figure out who your heroines are—whom you would most want to be like. That decided, figure out what is the unique quality that sets your model apart from others and then begin developing that same quality in yourself. Maybe it is selflessness or persistence. Love may be the pervading force. (Naturally, if your heroine is the mastermind of a crime syndicate, I recant this whole paragraph . . .)

Last, first, and always in your search for self, you must search for God. Faith may not come easily to you. You might even feel that it is forced upon you by the nature of your husband's vocation, making you resentful of God for putting you in this place. You can shout at the church for being evil and robbing you of your husband—even destroying your life. I did all that. It doesn't work. The only thing that works is to accept the life you have chosen, even if you didn't know what you were getting into, and come head on with the fact that it was your choice. Once the source of your condition is clearly identified, it becomes quite easy to worship God and to surrender your inner self to his keeping.

But why begin a book about living in the parsonage with self-searching? Frankly, because unless you've got your self and your soul in hand, you are in for big trouble. You are embarking on a lifetime of people who will variously love you; criticize you; use your money, your time, your talents; awe you with their brilliance—or their stupidity; stomp all over your emotions and never know it; control your income; choose your house; pick your furniture; tell you how to raise your kids. Any life experience you can think of, people will be involved in. You just don't spend a life with people well until you've checked out your inner resources. Knowing your self is the key to knowing others. It unlocks a lifetime of happiness for you, regardless of what vocation your husband is employed in because it lets you be you, secure in the knowledge that you are answering responsibly to yourself and God for your actions and words and nothing further is required. That way, if somebody else doesn't like what you're doing, you know it's his hang-up, not yours!

Oh, you'll make mistakes. But you'll correct them. You'll say the wrong thing, but you will be strong enough to apologize. You'll be dismayed, but reassurance will come. But you will also be natural, and people will feel at ease with you. You will share your happinesses, and others will know joy. You will love—and be loved. And best of all, to your own self you will be true. That's worth the whole self search.

So, in the words of my dad, go ahead—cast your bread upon the waters because it's sure to come back buttered!

2
In Sickness
and in Stealth

Love is the beginning and the end. Love is the ultimate relationship. Love is where it's at—and it better be where you're at if you live with a minister, because you're going to need all the love you can give.

A minister isn't an ordinary man—everybody knows that. The trouble is that *your* minister-husband keeps coming up super-ordinary at home. He burps at inopportune times. He picks his teeth. You always have to tell him what clothes to put together since his taste is atrocious. He yells at the kids—and even argues with you. No matter how you try to draw the picture, he just won't fit the stereotype. Hallelujah! He's a real man!

Problem: How do you help a real man fit into an unreal job?

Before you consider the solution—if there is one—you ought to know that by the time you finish this chapter you may be feeling sorry for yourself. In fact, you may feel absolutely neglected! Don't dismay. There are other chapters for you, but this one is for him. It presupposes that you really do love the dude and want like crazy to make his life easier—even richer and more interesting. So read with an open mind. Sometimes we women have to admit that part of our job is to care for and nourish our husbands regardless of the demands it places on us. (Women's libbers, skip to chapter 11.) An outside angle

to this approach is that he will love you to eternity—
maybe even through it—and you will feel of all women
most blessed. (No halo comes with the blessing, however.)

That understood, let's get back to the problem. Some
people believe there are three kinds of people in the
world: men, women, and ministers. The latter, by this
definition, are sexless, sinless entities more filled with
Spirit than spirits who go through life with blinders
that shield them from all the vicissitudes of worldly
struggles. Unfortunately, none of the above is true—
thank heavens! Can you imagine being married to a
sexless, sinless vegetable? Even *I* would vote for celibacy
if that were the case. It's unreal—but that's his job
description: unreal.

There is no other job on earth that expects a man to
work every possible waking moment, to comfort the
sick and dying, to be the tower of strength for the
bereaved and/or the anxious bridegroom, to counsel the
maritally afflicted, to pray at a moment's notice, to be
all-wise in the problems of child care and in-family
jousting, to administer a $50,000 budget, to raise money
for loan payments without issuing bonds, to run a
church program efficiently with an all-volunteer staff
that serves when it feels like it, to act as building and
grounds maintenance supervisor, to prepare miracu-
lously and preach eloquently, to dress meticulously but
not too well, to be a saint in all interpersonal relationships with language that even your grandmother couldn't
question, to love his children and see that they are raised
in an exemplary fashion, to keep his own marriage and
personal habits above question, to be never grossly (or
netly, either) in debt, and to set a pattern of living that

all can follow in personal faith and spiritual development. In case you have forgotten what I am talking
about, the above is the job description in abbreviated
form for the twentieth-century Man of God, commonly
known as minister.

Some of the ordinary tasks left out of the description
must be noted. He is also expected to relate to general
church committees, community service club and cham-
ber of commerce functions; to effect major social changes
in and around his parish; to bridge the generation gap
of the old and young so that they both get high on the
same thing—faith; to serve the senior citizens of the area;
to speak at commencements, dedications, installations,
and circle meetings; to drive the right car; to lead con-
gregational singing on key; never to get discouraged;
never to question his calling; to have an "in" with the
Boss; to provide all manner of duplicated material for
his congregation done on a machine that someone else
threw out; to answer to his superiors in such a way that
his parishioners are not ired; and to answer his parishioners in such a manner that his superiors do not become
suspicious. Meantime, *you* expect him to be a good husband, full of energy for recreation and fun; to share in
raising the children, including the everyday things like
putting them to bed occasionally or taking them for an
afternoon outing; to be a reasonable lover; to remember
your birthday and the in-law wedding anniversaries;
and not to schedule a potluck dinner on Valentine's Day.
Poor man!

No way can any man do all that and come off feeling
triumphant on every occasion. In fact, he may not manage a feeling of triumph more than a couple of times a
year. The rest of the time he sloshes back and forth

between satisfaction and depression or guilt. The options are all hard: he can take his choice of what he does well and specialize in it, letting all the rest of the tasks go; he can try to do them all and spread himself so thin that nothing is done well; he can add men to the staff who have strength where he is weak or not interested (money required here); he can collapse from exhaustion; or he can leave the ministry. Any of these choices is difficult, for all of them have their critics. More than any other job, the ministry requires a man to be sensitive to all human need, including his own, and have the hide of an elephant at the same time. He is surrounded by critics, but the only one he must deal with is the one inside himself.

Even as you must be true to your self to enjoy this life-style, he must make his peace with that person who dwells within. If Paul is his hero and he is constantly striving for perfection, he has to realize that he can't win *every* race. In fact, he has to choose which races to start in and then decide whether he will win, place, or show. This, of course, is where you enter the scene (but not with the starting gun). You are probably the only person who knows him well enough to see him as he actually is. Your handicap, however, is that you happen to be related to him through marriage and that sometimes clouds your perception. Well, wipe the fog of emotion away now and then, so you can see clearly with your head. That done, you are ready to be a helpmate in the truest sense of the word.

Task One: Know the content of his job, but don't try to do it for him—or even tell him how to do it unless he asks. Then offer your suggestions, but do not be personally offended if he does not use them or if he uses them and forgets to give you credit. (Love forgives, remember?) From the time he talks to you to the time the idea is put into action a lot of people will have become involved in it, added their own thinking, and changed it to fit the constantly shifting circumstances of people-work. Let him take the credit—praise warms the cockles of a man's heart and tides him over when his followers stand around while the cock crows . . .

Task Two: Be his lay person. How can he preach to people whose jobs are so different from his, who take weekends to go fishing while he is lucky to get a day off? Obvious. He lives with a wife who happens to be a lay member of the church who volunteers when she wants to and gets involved as much as she pleases—or as little. In short, you can be Super Lay Person. Even while you understand and give suggestions, you have got to stay as far removed from professional ministerial attitudes as you can. Be the Devil's Advocate at home. Prick in fun (or at least gently) the idealistic balloons he may tend to blow up so that he keeps his feet firmly on the ground where all the church members are also standing. Bring reality into his dreams with ideas that are positive and attitudes like those of the person who is outside the church thinking about coming in. To do this you must obviously know people like this. (It's good for your social life, too!) You must also have your ear to the ground so that you pick up clues to how people feel about certain things that are proposed. You will hear more than he will, but you must develop a Wisdom Strainer that only lets through the right things to your husband. The rest throw out with the garbage since that's what it is, or, if you are affected by it, develop a close confidant who lives Someplace Else.

The Third Task is much more fun: keep him well-balanced. Every man needs to be re-created occasionally, and if the first two jobs are difficult for you, revel in this one. Get hold of his schedule midway of the month and write yourself on before anyone else has the chance. Buy season tickets to something you both enjoy so that the dates are scheduled months before. Make sure they are inviolable. Encourage him to realize that without his presence your life is drab and depressing, that he is what puts the zing in your step, and, therefore, it is time the two of you stepped out. Give him time to escape at home with whatever satisfies him—the TV, books, the kids—and resist telling him during escape time that the women's society president is in the hospital. That will blow it all.

In fact, when he comes home, why not control the atmosphere? You can be the storehouse of humor which lightens his day. Any wife can greet her husband with the woes of her day or by demanding to hear what's troubling her beloved—but who wants to be just any wife? This is your chance to shine! Operate on all six senses. Let him smell something good when he comes through the door—even if it's only a cup of instant coffee (which, incidentally, takes care of the taste sense also). Then satiate his touch sense by the way you greet him with an unholy kiss. Satisfy his eyes with a reasonably straight house or a table that's set for dinner, or yourself aglow with the sharing of a sunset happening. And let him hear pleasant sounds, not nagging reproaches (save those for later when he's in the shower). Then, use your sixth sense to know what shape he's in. Listening to the way he walks into the house or how he shuts the door behind him may tell you a lot. So will the slump of his shoulders or the way he sighs as he sits down to dinner, or struggles to leave the table to go to a meeting. Unless you just can't—which will be a big part of the time—save your hassles for the times when he is feeling up.

Hassles there will be just because you are a family. He *does* have to know that Johnny wiped out the church treasurer's son in a fight at school today, that Frances has the flu and is running a 102-degree fever, that the baby has taken her first steps. Certainly he will also have to know that the kitchen drain is plugged solid, the curtain rods pulled out of the wallboard again today, and you only have fifty dollars to run on till the end of the month when today is the tenth. Probably while you're telling him all this lovely news, the baby will express her new ability to walk by demonstrating another newfound skill—and flush her shoe down the toilet (now you have forty dollars). Communicate you must, all this and more, but at least wait till after dinner . . .

A painless communication system that works for us is a chalkboard on which either of us writes the things that need doing around the house, and erase it when it is finished. The board does the nagging while we go on loving.

At some point along the path of understanding your husband, you may observe a strange closing action, not dissimilar to the turtle pulling into his shell when he thinks danger is near. This action may occur for many reasons. People may be criticizing him for a position he has taken. He may feel that you don't understand and don't want to. Perhaps he is confronted with a family situation that makes him feel a failure. He may

31

even be tired and have no way of coping with the need to rest. Here your sensitivity is supremely necessary. Now is the time for gentle prodding to help him talk out his inner brooding. Now is the time for extra ways to say "I love you." Now is the time to arrange dinner alone so that the two of you can search out what lies within each of you and share the hurt and care. If your husband is to do his job well, he must stay open to people, no matter how much it hurts. When he closes up, he shuts off himself and his love from those around him. And closing up or withdrawing is the easiest way to protect his self.

One or the other of you has to deal with the tired-minister syndrome. It is apt to occur at any time, but is contagious at Easter and Christmas. The high points of the church year may well bring your husband to the low point of his year. Easter Letdown is the big brother to Yearly Meeting Letdown, which is a cousin of Christmas Letdown, whose children might be named Thanksgiving, Pentecost, Epiphany, or End-of-Year. The job never ends. No sooner is one project finished than two more are waiting, and since the troubles of the world keep piling up around us, the temptation is to run faster just to stay in place. Great—until you start running down.

Your cajoling will be insufficient if you live with a driven man. About the only legitimate way such a man will rest is to get sick. Rarely does his congregation realize that demands exceeding his strength have put him in bed, but they do recognize illness since it visits their homes as well—often for the very same reason: the inability to say "no," quickly followed by the words "I have to rest this evening." The guilt of things undone is a dreadful driver. It should never be allowed to drive your husband—or you, for that matter.

But that is where we started, with realizing limitations. Sickness has a way of teaching us what we refuse to learn any other way, and since you took the pledge when you married him, now is the time for stealth! Sneak in the books he has been waiting to read. If he feels good enough, supply him with paper and pencil to write down that idea he has been dreaming about, or his paints for art therapy. If he feels the church must go on and he must be at the helm, let him communicate by tape recorder and minimum telephone, but connive with the church secretary to fend off all but absolute essentials. Even the President of the United States has a right to be sick. The difference is that he has a vice-president to take over, and your man may be alone. What a chance for the laymen to discover how to carry the load! Make no apology for such an opportunity for them, and in every way possible cover the bases so your husband can actually take time to get well. In sickness, use stealth— let that be your motto.

Throughout these pages you may notice that you have been given quite a big order. It may even sound as though you are supposed to give up your entire life for him. Not so. You would then become a nothing, a doormat. Instead, you need to be a very strong person who increases in wisdom and strength every day—and if you're not strong now, be encouraged. Nobody starts strong. You get that way a day at a time just the way all your church members do. You may arrive sooner because your days are fuller, but that can definitely be an advantage.

However, to satisfy your sense of neglect—and to be

perfectly honest—let me add that your standing up for
your rights as his wife and sweetheart is one of your
husband's needs. Sometimes you have to demand your
place in the sun. How else is your husband to learn how
to cope with the women he must work with if you are
not fully woman? If you feel neglected, say so. If you
feel unloved and he is unresponsive, tell him. If your
end of the burden is disproportionate, speak up! Chances
are that unless you do he will never notice that he is not
pulling his weight—nor would you if the case were
reversed. In no way should you become the submissive,
sainted martyr. Say what is on your mind—just try to
get your timing right! Five minutes before he is scheduled to leave for an officers' meeting is hardly the time
to burst into tears. At least wait until he gets home.
That may not be a good time either, but it's an improve-
ment. Besides, you will have thought of a lot more
material in the meantime . . .

Denying yourself is the same thing that he may be
doing, and two self-deniers make pretty boorish company. Your openness helps him to be open, so relax. Get
a load off your mind and figure you're educating your
husband at the same time. In fact, if you get the habit
of saying what is going on inside of you as it occurs,
you may find that you don't have any big showdowns
to go through. When that happens, you are actually approaching that nebulous thing called maturity. So find
your voice, put your mind in gear, and proceed with
reckless caution.

At some point in your husband's ministry you may
have to stand by and watch him get pulled apart. And
standing by is the best thing you can do—him, that is.
If you dearly love your man, your fighting instincts will

rear their ugly heads and you will itch to tell whoever is involved the error of their ways. Maybe the pulling will come from a higher source and involve a pulpit assignment which you see hurtful to your husband. Perhaps he is the victim of malicious gossip or of local politics. Of all the men in town he is the most vulnerable. If there is a time for closeness, this is it. Call out the rear guard! Now is the time to love him as though your very life depended on it—because it does. You are the only one he can turn to at a time like this. Just make the turning easier if you can. If you are weeping, at least weep together. In this and all other situations there is only one true recourse. Examine again your life in relation to God's will, and if peace is your reward, rest assured that whatever the outcome, God will be in it. You see, upholding your husband isn't a matter of pulling him up by his bootstraps; you're not strong enough for that! God-power is the secret! Without it, the whole thing comes tumbling down—your ministry, your marriage, your family—the whole show closes.

If your idea of being a good minister's wife is to push your husband to the top echelon of the church hierarchy, good luck! There aren't too many popes in the world, and virtually none in Protestant churches. Besides, a prerequisite for pope is celibacy, so your man doesn't qualify. If you married him to make his light shine, sometime or other you may have to come to terms with the fact that his light may extinguish slowly. You may not believe in predestination, but your man may not believe in politics either—and that may be what it takes to be Head Churchman. (Mind you, I could be wrong. This is only a clinical observation!) In fairness to Church Hierarchy, even *I* must admit that it isn't all politics. It could even be that the minister's wife is a victim of myopia—she loves her man so much that she can't see why the whole world doesn't recognize his greatness. But greatness is a relative thing (sometimes relatives help), and the world is full of great men. If you set your goals too high, your man will always feel like a failure in your presence and you will become the force that makes him work night and day. Result: you won't like the product you've made . . .

It is also important to realize that the product changes, as do you. One day you are young and ready to transform the church into the mighty giant for God you know it should be. A few fleeting years go by, and you discover that reality has made you accept the fact that God does things in his time, not yours. This is an especially hard concept for your husband to face, because at the same time his hair is beginning to turn white at the edges and the energy level has dropped a mite. He is definitely more experienced, but this could shift his polarity. Where once you had to dampen his idealism a little, now you may have to encourage him to have more of it. If a man thinks that nothing else will happen in the next twenty years before he retires, then rise to the occasion with an armful of dreams that you have been storing for just this moment. You need a long list of men who are fifty or more who are doing significant things in our world. Actually, most of the men who are world leaders are at least fifty, but this is seldom clear to a man when he hits his change-of-life-bottom-dropped-out-of-my-world days. Somewhere he probably read that if a man hasn't made it by the time he is thirty, he never will. Whoever wrote that dastardly sentence forgot to define what "making it" was (maybe he was just talking about sex!), so it lives on to haunt the egos of millions of men facing forty. Unfortunately, family expenses hit an all-time high at about the same period because your children are teen-agers involved in expensive school activities, launching into the world of automobiles and girl friends, wearing adult-priced clothes without adult-sized incomes to supply them. Forty can get pretty hairy. You look down the years and see an endless row of churches with you moving from one to the next until finally there aren't any more . . .

If you ever took a leap of faith, now is the time. A sabbatical may be the answer, or a try at a different kind of ministry. Even a move that boosts his ego can snap the doldrums, but whatever you do, change the pattern of life even if by little everyday things like going out to breakfast together once a week. Cheapest time to eat out I know of. Or meet him for a clandestine lunch in a special place. Convince him to update his wardrobe with something a little less preacherish even if it is only to go out with you. And check yourself. Maybe you are part of the cause. Have you let yourself get old and fat, without interest in the world around you? Are you Super Mother? If his sweetheart has disappeared, now is the time for you to rush to her aid. Shed those thirty pounds, delve into some new interests, or go back to school to acquire expanded brainpower. The new you could result in a renewed him!

Plan now to play later—that is, keep a retirement file. If you get to live that long, you will eventually join the ranks of the unemployed and underpaid. Look forward to it with ideas that sound like fun and stash them away for safekeeping. Periodically get them out and discuss them. You may find yourself retiring early this way, but that's a lot better than finally going to Athens and not being able to climb to the top of the Acropolis.

I once heard a minister's wife say upon retirement, "If I had it to do over, I would simply do more than I did." Being in my Resentment Period at that time, I thought she must surely be daft. Now her statement not only rings true but in practice reveals that the more you give of yourself, the more you receive from others— whether that more be love, material goods, or time.

All other things aside, when you give your husband love, you must also give him freedom—even to work himself to death if that is his choice. Set him free to do his thing. He only gets one life, so why not let him live it the way he feels is right for him? He, in turn, will give you freedom (if he doesn't, point out his error and assume said freedom). In spite of everything written on these pages, his ultimate happiness will be reached as the two of you learn to set the other loose in the world to be your own person, coming together to share your love and concern and going forth renewed again. As his wife, you can provide hope when things look hopeless, you can encourage faith when his foundations are threatened; but when it comes to love, you have to love him and leave him—to follow God his own way.

So if you throw away everything else in this chapter, at least keep this: love him! For God's sake, love him! Mind, soul, and (Paul permitting), body!

3
The Happy Hour

Mind, soul, and body! Well . . .

Maintaining a sex life in the parsonage is really a touch-and-go situation—you touch and he goes—to meetings, to preach, to call . . . And there you stand, all revved up ready to make love to your husband, but the CHURCH has stolen him away.

First error: the church did not take him; his job did. Also his natural dedication to work as a satisfying part of life, plus the commitment he has made to be in a certain place at a definite time. These are the things that took him away from you—not the church. Your problem is not to fight the church, but to teach your husband how to manage his sex life.

Seminaries are not the most scintillating advocates of sex. It is very difficult to write a paper on "The Existential Relationships of the Homophile" and get turned on! Theological libraries don't generally house many volumes on the sex life of the clergy, and scarcely a class is offered across the land on this exciting subject. Hollywood recognized this a long time ago with pictures like *Rain* and *Elmer Gantry*. Of course, they slanted the story so that the man was sex-starved, not merely deprived in his education and internship. Today's minister knows a great deal more than the cloistered past generations, but the problem is that he must practice what he preaches and has very little time to do so. He comes home emotionally drained and the phone keeps ringing, the doorbell chimes, the kids want to cram their whole lives into the thirty-five minutes allotted for dinner, and you are busy serving that dinner. Three hours later, after an administrative board meeting in which none of the projects he wanted received support, he is scarcely ready to be romantic.

Likewise, you have had your own heavy day, which is bound by a 7:30 A.M. school bus, a women's meeting, your part-time afternoon job, the grocery shopping, a load of wash, chauffeuring a son to the dentist, dinner, homework help, and the inevitable telephone. In order to survive you have now retired, which is fine with your preacher-husband because, at last (11:00 P.M.), he can have a few minutes of peace to unwind. If sex crosses his mind, it is with a promise for tomorrow morning.

The morning dawns bright and beautiful, but you are neither. Six-fifteen sounds the alarm. You shut it off quickly so as not to waken your tired husband, proceed with sending the children off to school, then settle down for a cup of coffee and the morning paper. At that moment your dashing lover appears—groping for a cup of coffee to spring him back into alertness. He has long forgotten the fleeting thought of the previous night, and from the looks of him it's just as well. By the time he has finished breakfast and come alive, you have finished the paper and are ready to start your day's work.

Then he remembers! You tremble on the threshold of decision, one eye on the clock. If you take time out for sex, will you make it to your first appointment? What will the church secretary think if he doesn't arrive on time? Does he have a meeting he has forgotten? Should you ask him?

You may not know it, but you stand at the crossroads that might eventually make or break your marriage. Before you answer, think! When else can you have sex? So you don't feel like sex now—so what? You will ten minutes from now. If you make an appointment for tonight with your husband, how can you be sure he will have any energy left? What about your own appointment? Well, sometimes it's fun to play "Beat the Clock." This is your big chance! Go ahead—take it!

Flexibility is the key to parsonage sex life. Without it there would be very few preacher's kids (or "theologian's brats," as my kids say). Without sex, sermons would dry up completely, counseling would be ineffective, and social engagements become devastatingly dangerous! So flexibility is a must. I'm sure a reigning monarch has the same problem and the same solution— take sex when you can fit it into the schedule, regardless of the time of day or night. Then, be innovative about making time in the schedule. An afternoon house call from your favorite minister-husband might be the solution—or a morning coffee break. You don't really have to drink the coffee. Or how about a "nooner"? Less resourceful but equally possible is setting the alarm clock for 3:00 A.M. That way, if you're a night person and he is a morning person, you have a happy compromise. It's still dark outside, but it actually is morning; besides, you will be too sleepy to notice . . .

Mood setting is another prime prerequisite in your husband's education. This must be a constant condition of living, public and private. Some call it openness to each other. To my way of thinking that is a very dull phrase to describe a very pleasant condition.

The right mood for sex is one that springs naturally out of affection. It is, however, very hard to be affectionate with someone who isn't there. Coupled with this difficulty is the fact that many men are not schooled in the life pattern of giving and receiving affection on a daily basis. They shook hands with their father when they left for college and gave their mother a perfunctory peck on the cheek. Granted, when your husband was dating you, he was much more attentive, perhaps even ardent in his affectionate pursuit—but that's what it was: pursuit. He has now caught and tagged you, so that part of the deal is over, and he tends to revert to affection accorded to someone halfway between girl friend and mother. Great! . . . if you want to be his affectionate mother, but lousy if you want to be his turned-on wife. So what to do?

The cure will take great patience. Remember it took some twenty or so years for him to develop his current habits, so don't expect to undo it in a day—or even a year for that matter. My current husband (he's the only one, but he is still current) required three years to accomplish this learning, totally unaware that he was learning at all. Simply put, I refused to let him be anything but affectionate by constantly putting my arms around him, plopping into his lap at odd moments, holding his hand the way we did when sweethearts, nibbling at his ear—all the usual things. At the end of three years I decided I had done enough, so I quit. Completely. Overnight. My poor husband couldn't figure out what had happened. Was I all right? Did I feel well? Fine, was my reply. About the third day (traditional for awakenings) he arose from the breakfast table, came over to me, and kissed me on the cheek. Shades of mother! I hung on though, and by afternoon he held me in his arms for a moment on the way to his study. Progress! By nightfall he was downright passionate. I encouraged all but initiated none of the action. Several weeks later we had settled down to a lifelong pattern of touching each other with affection. In fact, when our heads and tongues separate us, the one rule stands: keep touching. It will bring you through many difficult days when you may feel estranged from each other. The three years were all worth the time—and fun, too!

Feeling sorry for yourself, pouting, or generally adopting a "poor me" attitude is the quickest way to turn a man off. Who wants to make love to a kid sulking in the corner? Your preacher is a man, and he'll be attracted to the poised, dashing woman anytime over the crying child. So throw out the tissue box and make yourself interesting. Tap your inner wealth, and you won't be poor anymore.

The word "public" crept in with regard to affection. Discretion is the key word. Communion may be a love feast, but it is hardly the time to kiss your husband! A hand clasp, honest and not for anyone else's benefit, can say volumes—both to each other and to your parishioners. In this day of broken homes it is reassuring to know that someone still cares about his or her aging spouse. You certainly don't need to talk about your sex life to accomplish an awareness of your love, but neither do you have to ban everything personal from your conversations.

For instance, one Sunday morning after worship a

little lady in her seventies approached me with a question about a certain activity that was to take place in the church involving her women's group. I didn't happen to know anything about it and said so, whereupon she became very indignant. Hadn't my husband told me? When I replied in the negative, her eyes flashed as she threw out her final question, "Well, what *do* you talk about when you're together?" Smiling (I hoped kindly) I answered, "Well, usually we don't talk. We just make love!" When her eyebrows had come down, a crooked smile worked its way up one side of her face, and she said, "I guess that would be more fun, wouldn't it?" We have been friends a long time now because she was able to recognize in my answer a very human experience (which she once had shared) and the humanness of our home life. I definitely do not recommend that you apply the above illustration in your parish. Let's face it—I was lucky that time! Find your own way to be open with and about affection, and then move on to awareness.

Put succinctly, a minister's wife—or any wife for that matter—needs to be aware of her husband's burdens, and your husband probably carries more than his fair share. Not only is he in a position to know and take leadership about most of the social problems of our society, but he deals with those problems among the members of the very same families he preaches to on Sunday. And that is what he has been doing when he comes home to you. It may not be enough to be affectionate or flexible. You have a bigger challenge on your hands. He may stand in need of an honest-to-goodness R and R (rest and recreation).

The simplest kind of R and R can be contrived at

home. Invite in a few close friends *outside* the church, people you can let down your hair with, serve plain food to, and not dress up for. Plan a gentle evening of talk, food, and music to end when it feels like it. This is legitimate as an evening on the calendar, for guests are universally regarded as important. If having people in is not your thing, then do the opposite; go out to dinner, take in a local happening—an art show, a college play (make sure it's a comedy), a high-school basketball game where your kids attend. Anything that takes his mind off his work is likely to refresh him so that *you* can catch his attention. Besides, he needs the break; and even if your sex life is fantastic, you still should help him take a refresher evening now and then.

Another *modus operandi* requires a bit more planning and money unless you have someone who will lend you a cabin in the mountains. For this R and R you must have a sitter for your children as you must go alone. No fooling around with a coffee-break approach. This is an out-and-out sex break. Two days—or even twenty-four hours—away at some undisclosed place works wonders. An off-season visit to the seashore finds prices down and the shore empty—a delightful place to walk hand in hand, talking about your life together and the future of your family unit. Even one night at a motel within a ten-mile radius can give you a lift by its very secretiveness. It has all the adventure of a rendezvous, creates an attitude of expectation, and stirs up fire in the old boy.

A slightly more drastic recommendation can also have delightful results. Let him take a week of his vacation alone. If he likes to ski, let him. Sail? Encourage it. Hunt? Pack for him. Kiss him goodby happily (even if you don't feel like it), and then settle down to a week of pampering yourself as well. Sleep a little more. Don't cook as much. Let the house slide a little. Do things *you* want to do. By the end of the week you'll find yourself looking forward to his return with expectation, so clean the house, wash your hair, and look your best. When he comes through that door, greet him as though he had been gone a year, and chances are he'll treat you likewise.

If nothing so far has worked, you are definitely in trouble. Maybe the problem is that you're too serious about the whole thing. Sex should be fun, not a duty— or a dirty, for that matter. Examine *your* attitude. Perchance do you think it's not proper for a minister's wife to enjoy sex? Then just drop the first word because that is where the trouble lies. You are not a minister's wife. You are the wife of a man who happens to be a minister. Now that's a different show. If you tend to wear long skirts or navy blue and black, medium heels in Oxford styles, hair neatly tucked in a bun at the back, then face it: YOU are the problem. It may be intriguing to entice a prude into bed once, but after finding out that her prudery goes clear to the center of her being, even the most ardent lover will give up.

The bedroom is the most honest place to let yourself go. If you are truly hung up on wearing black, then wear black lace, unlined. Take your hair out of the bun and brush it—nude (you, not the hair)—in the presence of your husband, of course. Learn to laugh at yourself and your image. The switch from public to private is ridiculous anyway, so why not laugh?

Meanwhile, assure your mate that sex is a real tension relaxer and excellent for exercise. It makes one's heart beat faster and is more pleasant than jogging. Explain to him that such experiences will give him true empathy in counseling and in understanding the whole human race. Murmur something consoling in his ear like, "There now, doesn't that feel better than skiing?" or "Doesn't this beat going to that old meeting?" Be careful with the latter question, though, for it may raise work-guilt, which must be kept to an absolute minimum for sexual moments.

There are a few specific problems one must deal with in the parsonage. One of these is the telephone. It has a way of ringing at the most inopportune moment. You know, there you are making love to your husband and the phone rings. The voice on the other end is identified as the local radio station wondering if you would be willing to do a noon talk-show on women's liberation! Try taking the phone off the hook. This gives you a few minutes of uninterrupted freedom before the operator starts blowing the whistle for you to hang up. At this point you can either develop instant deafness or push the button down momentarily for another few minutes. This is not recommended, however, for it tends to distract.

If you cannot bring yourself to leave the phone off because you're on a party line or because of the waves of guilt that pour over your husband, and if you cannot convince him that the real emergency is occurring inside you, then you must resort to other devices. Be prepared in case the phone rings: let it ring at least four times so when your husband answers, his labored breathing is easily explained by the caller: "Oh, I've made you run to the phone! I'm *so* sorry." No explanation is necessary.

Best of all, invest in a plug-in telephone . . . and pull the plug! Instant peace!

Coitus interruptus occurs for other reasons as well—

the kids, the dog, the doorbell. These problems should not be taken personally, but experientially. They happen to every married couple, so figure you are building your own marriage folklore and laugh at them. Get a good lock for the bedroom door, put the car in the garage for a change, send the kids to the store or the movies, and put the dog out. Planning always improves performance!

Why a whole chapter devoted to sex? Is it really that important? Well, not any more important than the other chapters, perhaps, but a mite more difficult to work into the schedule and a shade more apt to be slighted by two people who lead fantastically busy lives and may take a perfunctory attitude toward the subject of procreation. All kinds of taboos still exist about this ancient human relationship, especially within the church walls. Many of us, self included, believe that sex belongs within marriage, an attitude that is almost heretical in some segments of our society. Further, ministers tend to look for wives who come from church homes with strong moral teachings. The problem is that sometimes those same homes forget to teach that sex is not only an expected but a joyful part of marriage, to be entered into eagerly and with great love. If a couple comes into the ministry with hang-ups about sex already established, their private life is in for harder times than that of people in other professions because the pressures are almost all emotional. This tends to suck out the life that might be present; and along with the life the minister must constantly be giving away, a parsonage marriage has a much greater chance of drying up.

There is also the ever-present danger of the alluring female. She may not look very ravishing but, if your sex life is nil, she doesn't have to. Every day you send your husband out to call on the widowed and divorced, the woman whose husband "doesn't love her," or the secretary who may offer him far more patience and understanding than you do. Face it! Women are a ministerial job hazard. He sees them in their most help-less conditions, begging for a man to depend on. He comforts them at their most susceptible moments, when a loved husband is gone or a hated one has walked out the door. Unwittingly, he pays attention to a woman who works in the church while, unknown to him, her life is empty and meaningless. He is startled to hear one day that she believes herself to be in love with him—and what should she do? So it's one against a million—you against them.

It doesn't have to be, though, and shouldn't be. It should be you *with* them: loving them, understanding their hurts, comforting and giving help to them, and keeping your husband safe through it all.

And that is where sex comes in. The old adage that a satisfied man seldom notices other women happens to be a good gamble. A husband who is well loved and physically satisfied is much better equipped to deal with other men's wives as persons rather than as women. A healthy parsonage sex life (with you, of course) keeps his perspective straight. Seen that way, one chapter on sex seems too short?

There is a bonus to these pages. A *healthy* sex life keeps your love fresh and glowing. One sure sign at our house that the two of us need to become one is when we get short and crotchety with each other. Afterward, we find tensions lessened and understanding easier to come by. Mind you, it is not a cure-all; and if sex is approached as a duty, it is a cure-nothing. It might even make things worse.

Attitude is everything. Sex, like all other human functions, is God-given. So receive it like one of his children, which you are. Enter into the experience with joy and thanksgiving—joy that you can know such exquisite emotions and thanksgiving for such a wonderful husband, healthy, strong, and able. And if he's not so able, help him a little . . .

After all, every one of us has the potential to become a first-rate Under-cover Agent!

4
The Insufferable Little Children

Satisfied lovers, beware; for sooner or later you may have an insane urge to have a baby! The ego strains to form a replica of itself, to find out what combination of genes you actually have, to procreate the race and overcrowd the earth. Sometimes you don't get the pleasure of actually thinking all of this—you just find yourself pregnant one day. After cursing or blessing Eve for swallowing that apple seed long ago, you are probably inclined to settle in for the long haul—and is it going to be long! Twenty years later I'm still waiting for my oldest to get his education and be self-supporting.

Thanks to the coming of the Pill we have a little more choice of how many "pills" we will have, and that is definitely an economic blessing! A wealthy young couple in one of our early churches was commenting on the size of our family (then it was three) and was reeling from the shock that I intended to make it four. They informed me that they had decided they could only afford two. My idealism came to the fore, and I announced grandly that there simply weren't enough Christian leaders in the world and this was what I intended to provide. Through the years that statement has tempered somewhat—my children will definitely be leaders, but their causes may be something else!

Your new cause-and-effect will probably become a

cause célèbre when the word gets around. A baby in the parsonage—*before* it comes—is considered a church event, especially if there hasn't been one for years. Hallelujah for church people who literally have fed, clothed, cared for, saved the life of, and put up with my children! They will surely be recognized on Judgment Day with a special award. It all began with the showers —nobody had such showers. The bed came from the women's society, the night circle provided the bathinette, the whole church celebrated with clothing galore, including a clothespin apron for my husband. (I wonder if I sent them all thank-you notes?)

The message should have been clear, but I missed it: WE were having a baby. Every grandmother felt the stir in her ample bosom, every mother had to examine the new product for flaws, the men wanted to test it for balance and agility by tossing it into the air—and I wanted them to leave my baby *alone!* To me it seemed they held it just long enough to make it cry and then gave it back. (Actually, "it" was a him, in case you are wondering.) The baby survived, however, and the novelty wore off when he approached the age of loud sounds in the middle of the worship service or escaped my clutch to upset the flowers on the altar after the service. Slowly the congregation settled down to suffer in silence as I tried to learn how to control my offspring.

Teaching reverence (interpret as silence and good manners) to your child is not quite so simple in the parsonage as it is for the parishioner. His child may come into the church building one or two hours a week and even experience awe at the uniqueness of things that happen there. He might confuse your husband (complete with clergy apparel) with something resembling his idea of God. Naturally, he behaves! No such luck for you. That guy in the front is good old Dad, who loves to play horsey on the living room floor and to whom you can talk anytime—so why is this time different? Dad is often surrounded by lots of people, so the natural thing is just to take cuts in the line. And, of course, Dad prays at home and is very proud that he has taught his son to say "Amen," so why should he be surprised when the son stands up during the pastoral prayer and calls loudly, "Amen, Daddy, Amen"?

If you happen to live next door to the church, the building is as familiar as home—maybe more so. It is a very interesting place with lots of people going in and out, a natural attraction to a growing young mind just learning communication skills. So maybe twenty hours of the week your child spends in the church building, and you expect him suddenly to change his concept of how to act there for one hour on Sunday? That is a very complex task, especially considering that some of the adults have yet to figure out that, when *they* go to church, they should quit talking when the organ begins. The task is virtually impossible!

Running a close second in impossibility is living in a house where all the furniture belongs to the church. How do you tell a two-year-old not to cut his teeth on the dining room table because it belongs to the church, and the parsonage committee won't understand? Simple. Since he can't understand and the hang-up about furniture belonging to the church is in your head, you stop him the very same way the parishioners do when their kids chew on the furniture. With emphatic discipline! Care of property is a very difficult concept for the young child to grasp, especially if yours has never been cared for in the first place—or if your yard is the churchyard and your child's toys are taken over by the church school children every Sunday. You do what you can and leave the rest till you move from that place. You get more than one chance to teach the finer disciplines—the trick is to use every chance you get.

Meantime, your child—or children as it quickly may become—will be teaching *you* a lot of things. Take perspective, for example. Coming down the aisle of the church with the choir one morning, I spied a pew totally empty except for my small son. I knew there were people standing at the back of the church, and the red flag went up in my brain. Later it was revealed that my four-year-old had told everyone who started to sit there that this was his pew and no one else was allowed! Immediately, we had a new perspective—about our son, our church people who had gone along with the thing, and our need to communicate personal relations more clearly. We even had to tell the ushers that they should not have played along with his demands—which they thought were hilarious. And I learned about letting a four-year-old sit alone in church . . .

Vigilance is another tremendous gift your offspring will cause you to develop. When your daughter sits down on the front-porch steps and proceeds to unclothe herself entirely, you become more watchful. Then, when you find your barely walking son standing atop the water box of the toilet and hanging onto the window ledge above so that he might see out, you get downright over-cautious. But when that same son, nine months later, takes literally the suggestion that he go ride his tricycle and you and the church members finally find him four hours later about to cross the busiest intersection in your city—still on his tricycle—you learn the full meaning of the word "vigilance"!

Close on its track will come a lesson about self-determination. You encourage your child to be independent, to conquer skills so that he has a good feeling about himself, and then one Sunday you can't find him anywhere after church. The search is in vain, so you finally go home with a nagging thought that maybe (it couldn't be!) he has walked home. Sure enough, standing triumphantly on the front lawn is your three-year-old, who has walked a mile and a half under freeways and past stoplights, and fairly glistens with pride. "I came home all by myself!" That is a hard one to put down. You might as well face it. All a parent gets to do is put in a little guidance now and then.

Take toilet training, for instance. Since your child is apt to go more places and see more buildings than the average child, trying to acquaint him with the restroom facilities and convince him that he should use them can be a monumental task by itself. The seat isn't shaped right or the paper cover is a curiosity object or the emphasis suddenly gets shifted so that you begin to wonder if your youngster has a urinary tract problem. One trip we took across the United States we dubbed "The John Tour" since our youngest would scarcely get into a restaurant or public building before going on a search for the men's room. When he made repeat visits to some of them—three times during a meal—we began to question him. From then on, we got a complete description of the entire facility, often including the shape of the water faucets and the design of the wallpaper.

Such innovations in training experiences have their

good points, however. After weeks of trying to get our son to stand up like a man, he finally got caught without his beloved johnny-seat and discovered he could perform in an upright position. That conquered, he quickly progressed to aim control—a point of training the books hadn't mentioned . . .

As your child grows in stature and (you hope) in wisdom, he will have many lessons in humility for you. Stay home sick with the flu, and he will surely acolyte in his oldest paint-smeared jeans with the torn knee! Or stay too late at an evening meeting and you may spy him kneeling at the altar, whereafter he will announce loudly, "Thank goodness, that's done! At least I won't have to say my prayers when I get home!" About that point you will begin to wonder who is supposed to be increasing in wisdom, and you may find a fast upswing in your devotional life as you make a crisis call for help.

Someplace along the way the child will discover that he has a name other than his given one. A title, if you will. He is "The Preacher's Kid." A little research on his part will turn up all manner of interesting things that everybody knows but him. Preachers' kids fight more, swear more, talk back more, neck more, and generally raise more hell than any other kind of kid. You desperately need to protect him from this vital information, since he may decide to live up to his reputation! Counter it with truth: that ministers' sons contribute a disproportionate amount of leadership in our country, often rising to high offices in the government, presidencies of universities and businesses, and are heavily represented in *Who's Who*. The difficulty is that he may not remember this when some other kid is yelling "Look at the sissy!" because he refuses to fight. You have to help him find a happy balance between the two extremes, so that *he* can be happy.

Meantime, he may be feeling slightly apprehensive about people. Moving tends to make the young child (and the older one, too!) wonder if it is really safe to make close friends since he may move away from them next year. New schools become a terrifying place because so few faces look familiar, and your child may begin to feel that the only safe place is in the family. That decided, he withdraws to home base and stays there. You may be feeling a little lost yourself and are hard put to help him find companions; but find you must, for however fragile you feel, your child is a hundred times more frightened of the outside world.

Cub Scouts and Brownies—with you helping or leading—are great ways to give your child friends and security all at the same time. Every den mother is a heroine to the boys she works with, and you have provided a natural invitation for them to know your child. If that's not your thing, encourage your children to bring their friends home and then make it a pleasant place to be when they arrive. Overnight visits also strengthen relationships.

It is also important that your child understand that moving doesn't happen just to him. Our mobile society shifts fathers at will back and forth across the country often with greater frequency than your husband is moved, giving you a chance to teach your child how to care about a friend who is leaving and how to receive someone new in the area. Even while I was writing this, my youngest son's friend called home to check in with his mother only to learn that his father had just informed the family that they were moving to another state some

2,000 miles away. It was the sixth move for this boy of eleven.

School shifts within a town must be counted as moves even though home stays still. If, in one pastorate, your child moves from elementary to intermediate school and then gets caught in a district realignment, he will have been in three schools in five years. Maybe he started school someplace else and then you are moved, giving him a grand total of five schools in six or seven years. Granted, he is brilliant, but it may not always show on his record and it would help if you showed a little mercy through it all . . .

The passage of time being inevitable, that little baby whom everyone welcomed with open arms will become a teen-ager, and now the real challenge begins—for both of you. Also at this time your husband may be going through his end-of-the-road syndrome, you may be entering your menopause, and both of you are slightly worse for wear! You may even be wondering if this child will *ever* turn into a person. With luck, there's hope— but the state of your home and the attitude of openness that exists between you and your children will never be more crucial. Peer pressure being what it is, your teen-ager may feel the whole world is peering—right into his private life. If P.K. (preacher's kid) hadn't caught up with him before, it surely will now (even in this enlightened day), and he has to come to terms with it. Lucky is the parsonage child who has the foresight to identify those around him as engineer's kids, doctor's kids, etc. and know that it is just a tag, not a command. That knowledge, however, may not save him from being caught in a power struggle between two organizations in the church who want the minister's son in *their* group.

One of our children is still recovering from such an experience, and three years later is just beginning to attend church again. If ever they needed a buffer, the time is now—and you're it!

You can't be a buffer if you are more concerned with saving your own skin. If your daughter gets pregnant, you can hide her away and fabricate many stories to cover her absence, you can face abortion as the answer, or you can stand beside her in her decision to keep her child. None of it will be easy, but she must have the same right of decision allotted to every other teen-ager and you must go on living. If you think only about what the church will say or how it will affect your husband's ministry, you have forgotten your daughter—and she is the one in trouble. She is your first concern. Chances are you will not only survive, but you may discover a new empathy with people in the congregation who have been through similar problems and are anxious to console you in your time of need.

Perhaps the problem won't be so obvious—just obnoxious. Try long hair and a motorcycle for openers. Do you let him come to church that way or do you tell him that unless he dresses properly he is not to show? If yours is the second choice, rest assured: he won't show for a long, long time. A teen-ager naturally vacillates between independence and acquiescence. Yours is no different. And unless you've been able to help him separate the difference between his father (who is also his minister) and his own spiritual life, he may use his independence to embarrass his father and to rebel against his authority. Rebellion is commonplace to the teen-ager anyway. It's just harder to live with for all people involved when you belong to a family that stays more or less in the public view. (The "more or less" depends on the size of your parish and/or community, and how much *you* keep everybody informed of what's going on in your family!)

Rebellion can take a much more subtle form: "I'm not going!" Please think on those words. They have echoed around the world of churchgoing families for eons. All your members with teen-agers have heard them. Husbands have stayed home because wives said those words, and vice versa. You are *not* in a national crisis, so don't react as though bombs are falling. Sometimes I don't feel like going to church, and sometimes my kids don't feel like going. Force them, you say. Sure—right out the church door! Teen years are the time for thinking about things, deciding who the person inside is, figuring out how much freedom one can handle, and testing the parental foot to see how hard it comes down. Many are the almost-adults who have used the ploy of not going to church only to discover the parents aren't threatened all that much, so they move on to some other tactic which gets more action and quietly go back to church.

Consider, too, that your husband's church is not the only accepted path to the promised land. If things are too uptight around home and church, point out a congregation that your child might enjoy being a part of. Oh, I know somebody will gossip about it, but that's his problem. *Your* problem is to see that your husband understands such a move and is not threatened by it. Besides, how better can he learn what his competition is up to than to have an insider in his own house?

Somewhere in all of this you have to give God a chance, too. I mean, how *do* you expect to do all this by

yourself? Just maybe there is a plan for your child's life
and you can trust the Creator to work it out, with only
a little assist from you in the crunch? Instead of con-
demning the wayward son, talk about what a great thing
happened today (for your sake, I hope some great things
happen!) or how really meaningful worship is to you.
But don't overdo it. Just enough is the key—you have
to determine how much is enough.

Are you ready to learn courage? empathy? faith? The
teachers have strange names—straight out of *Time
Magazine* or your local Free Clinic. The words strike
terror in the hearts of parents everywhere: narcotics,
abortion, premarital sex, trial marriage, drifting. Companion words raise a lump in the throat of some—like
long hair, own apartment, boyfriend with a curtained
van, smoking, alcohol. Whee—what a job our grand-
mothers didn't have! A generation is making its own
rules, and your child is right in the middle of it. So don't
panic. All the parishioners' children are right in it, too.
Chances are they are hiding some mighty big skeletons in
their closets right now that come out at night to haunt
them and to ask, "What did you do wrong?" The answer
is so simple: nothing, if you loved and directed your
child in the best way you know. The best tool you have
to give your teen-ager is faith in God and loyalty to
himself and his family. But regardless of what you have
given, these problems might come to your family. Then
you will know what your husband has been preaching
about all these years: Hell. And when all the weeping
is done, you are right back where you started—you have
to trust in God.

Now, before you go into a fast swoon and/or enroll
your daughter in a convent, let us hurry back to that

original statement—that P.K.s rank heavily on the side of leadership, high office, and significant contributions to society. That is where most of our adored children will come out: living happy, satisfied lives, being productive members of society. The most traumatic thing you may have to endure is The Wedding, and the most important thing to keep firmly in mind is *whose* wedding it is.

If you get the feeling that the church just somehow is always involved in your decisions, you may be right. It certainly can be if you let it. The degree of involvement is strictly up to you, though, and The Wedding may be the supreme test of your ability to control the involvement. Let us assume that you have served your current church for six years, bringing with you a gangling daughter of thirteen. She has grown up in that community and church. Some people almost consider her a part of them. One day she returns home for a quick weekend from college with a young man she has written about a time or two. Brace yourself! Not only do they want to get married, but they have set the date, planned the details, and have decided not to have more than twenty-five guests. Just yesterday someone had said to you that she was *so* looking forward to the time when your daughter would be married—she would make such a beautiful bride. Then your friend had added that she knew just what she wanted to give her . . .

Now, one day later, here sits your beautiful daughter telling you she doesn't want any of the church people to come. Just relatives and a few close friends. Big weddings are such a fake! And they could get by without all those wedding presents—they just clutter up your life with materialism, keeping you from being truly free. "Don't you think so, mother? Isn't it wonderful? And you won't have to do a thing! It's almost all done because we knew you would love whatever we wanted." Your mind flits back to your own dreams for her wedding, you remember how your husband has rejoiced that he could perform the ceremony—and you hear her saying that this boy beside her has the neatest minister who will do the ceremony so that Daddy can just give her away. You suddenly have a fit of coughing . . .

Cheers, old girl, and welcome into the Society of Disappointed Mothers. Their members can tell you tales of cajoling, arguing, crying, pleading—all to no avail (except that the wedding happiness was greatly dimmed by their efforts). You and your husband can fly united through this scene, demanding that the wedding be in the church and everyone be invited—you might even win. The question is, what? Just maybe this is the wedding your daughter has always secretly dreamed about but never had enough courage to explain until she found her man to support her. Why take away her dream? How much better to announce to the congregation by word or church paper that Jody and Bill have decided to be married in a small family wedding and will be living at such and such a place. Sure, a few people will buzz, some will be disappointed; but they'll get over it and so will you.

If the choice is theirs to have a full-scale Cecil B. DeMille production, expect help—and welcome it. For a long time those who volunteered will remember the occasion with pride, delighted that they were a part of it. Expect it to be exhausting. So what—you can rest later. Enjoy the now!

One morning several weddings later you will wake up to the fact that it is terribly quiet in the parsonage. Then you remember—you are resting up from your *last* wedding. No more P.K.s to hassle you, only the preacher himself. You got them safely through it all. The phone rings. Well, you thought you got them safely through it all . . .

The separated life that some theologians talk about wasn't supposed to refer to this period of your life, but it could. With children far away you have new freedom to follow your own pursuits, to enjoy your husband, to take a more active part in all of life, separated at last from your children. That is, until the phone rings. Once a mother, always a mother, and about to be a grandmother. Shades of rocking chairs and crochet hooks! You fly about the country or travel to the next town to lend a hand when you can, but the beautiful thing is that you have so much to do when you live in the parsonage, so much always happening, that you can—perhaps—let go of your children more easily than the woman whose life is empty when they leave. And again, you have to trust God to care for them when you no longer can, to show them the way to happiness because your direction won't be wanted very much now.

You've learned a lot! Perspective, vigilance, self-determination, humility, courage, empathy, faith. You have suffered through the insufferable little children—not on your life, you didn't! If suffering is what you have been doing for years, you failed the course. You should have been laughing, crying, sharing, dreaming, helping—and above all, loving. That way the next entry in *Who's Who* might start with the same last name as yours!

5
Love Thy Neighbor

If you have reached this far in your reading, you are almost halfway through—but not halfway home. Unless you happen to be born with a nine-foot halo and spout forth angelic utterances that cause people to fall at your feet in awe, chances are that the tough assignment begins now—learning to love the church people.

More aptly put, learning to love people is a lifelong adventure, and some of us are more adventurous than others. The particular people you are concerned with happen to be people who go to church, but not all of them are church people. Some of them are fringe people —like the fringe on your husband's stole, they simply decorate the garment. These people require little more than a friendly smile and warm handshake since more than that may scare them away altogether. *Church* people are something else . . .

Definition of church people (mine): The people who concern themselves with the inner workings and ongoing structures of the organization and life of any religious body. They come in all shapes and sizes, with warm and cold hearts, educated and ignorant, kind and critical, spiritual and agnostic. The most desired are of even mental balance, not using the church for an ego trip where they can be Director-in-Charge-of-Everything. A few must be classified Saint with a few also earning the title of Devil's Advocate. In short, church people are a collection of all the people in the world with one big plus: they are searching to be better tomorrow than they were yesterday.

Your immediate task is to realize that they have not yet arrived at their goal—and, incidentally, neither have you or your husband. Facing your own inadequacies along with knowing your husband's strong and weak areas is an absolute prerequisite for coping with the intimacies of the inner church.

Let's first clarify one fine point. You are not the only woman who lives in the public eye. And I am definitely not talking about Hollywood stars or presidents' wives. There are thousands of women across the nation who are married to psychiatrists, doctors, educators, lawyers, all of whom feel they must live circumspect lives or they will hurt their husband's livelihood. Their children feel the pressure as do yours. The teacher's kid is supposed to be smart, the psychiatrist's kid had better be mentally stable, the doctor's kid ought to stay healthy at least, and the preacher's kid should behave himself. (So much for old wives' tales!) You and your family are not alone in handling the feelings of many eyes watching. The question is—what are you going to do with that feeling?

Paranoia is definitely not the answer. One minister's wife moved to the second story of the house and stayed there. Wrong solution. Equally wrong is that temptation to be perfect which we talked about in chapter one: you, your husband, your children, the dog, the cat, the house, the yard, the way you dress, the desserts you serve, the car you drive—the list is absolutely endless! If Paul couldn't attain perfection, how in the heck do you expect to make it? You're not even Jewish!

Another imperfect solution is to make your family your whole life. In this day of Women's Lib, you are probably reading that sentence wrong. What I mean is that your family becomes the mainstream of your existence to the exclusion of close friends, good social times, natural releases of a recreational and group nature. Excluding these things keeps you protected because people see very little of your real self, but it also narrows your life until you might as well be dead—and you probably are, inside!

A very popular way to solve the fish-bowl syndrome is total flight. Let me first state that I am employed full-time and fully recognize the financial and emotional needs of the parsonage that cause a woman to work. However, employment and/or career development *can* be a way of escaping, pure and simple. This may work well for awhile but, if the problems that drove the woman to escape are not faced and handled, the husband will soon feel alone and despairing. Many a man leaves the ministry today because of the tug-of-war going on at home. If you work, try to remember you are still a part of the Support Team.

So how to cope? Rule One: keep your head in charge, not your heart. Living in the parsonage *is* different from living in the doctor's or educator's home. You are integrally involved in the lives of the people your husband works with, often when you would rather not be. They come to your door, they call on your phone, they come visiting when you have nothing much to eat and it's dinner time, or when you're washing your hair, or when your kids are sick and running around in torn pajamas, or when you're trying desperately to finish a special dress for your daughter and you haven't touched the house all day. Let's face it—you are exposed. Like it or not, that's the way it is.

There are degrees of exposure from parish to parish. Be thankful you don't live in Samoa where the only guest house in town is the parsonage, so everybody goes there when he doesn't feel like living at home. In the States, things are simpler. Your house may be next door to the church, but the odds are growing that it will be four blocks or four miles from the church. Excellent idea! You become another family on the street. All your church members know where you live, but now they come when they have a reason to come. Good and bad —you gain privacy but lose frequent contact, and it becomes more difficult to know everyone. Still, it can help. The problem comes when you have no control over the location; you simply live in the house that's there. Hence, the solution that works now may not even be applicable the next time you move.

So back to Rule One. It's what is in your head that counts, i.e., your attitude. Are you open or closed? No one promised you a rose garden, but even rose gardens have thorns. They also have beautiful blossoms and heady fragrance. You may have to grow past the thorns in order to produce the rose. Staying open to people regardless of the cost is the only real way. Your emotions will make you one day warm and the next day cool, according to how you feel. It is absolutely essential to act on what you know, and there is a lot to know.

No one will have to teach you that it hurts when someone criticizes you, your husband, or your children. You probably learned that just growing up. Now you must learn how to resolve criticism so that it does not destroy you. I live by the motto "This, too, shall pass," but that's not enough. There is no joy living that way. The key is to understand.

As a young wife of twenty-two, I often wore shorts on hot days (not hot pants, mind you, just shorts). The house happened to be next to the church, but, since I wore them only at home and in my own backyard, I thought nothing of it. One Sunday morning I complimented a woman of the church on her earrings, commenting that I had almost purchased a similar pair but my mother had deterred me with the statement that they were something a minister's wife shouldn't wear. To me the whole thing was a little amusing, but I had honored my mother for the moment. The woman suddenly drew herself up, her eyes almost popping out of her head, and exploded with, "Well, I know something a minister's wife shouldn't wear—SHORTS!" She fairly snorted the word, then went into a long tirade about men's apparel not being worn by women, etc., etc., finally concluding with the statement that she hoped *her* daughter would never wear them. I cried all afternoon, even though I had managed to say quietly that, when it was hot, that was what I liked to wear. Several years and lots of experience dealing with people passed before it hit me one day what her problem had been. She must have weighed three hundred pounds; her daughter was almost six feet tall and weighed at least two hundred fifty. Suddenly, I could laugh and forgive, and even agree with her—I hoped her daughter would never wear shorts either! If only emotion had been pushed out of the way so that understanding could have taken place, how much easier it would have been.

Learning how to talk is also helpful. Being of the foot-in-mouth variety, I envy the gracious woman, always tactful, saying precisely the right thing at the right moment. Oh, the agony of the spoken word followed by exquisite silence! In any case, *never* compromise your inherent person just to be what somebody else wants you to be. The price is too great. Tongue control can be learned though, and silence really *is* golden sometimes. You may wish later you had cut your tongue off anyway, and that is a terrible way to control your speech. Put your head in gear instead.

Getting your perspective right is also essential. Most of us want to see everything from *our* point of view. Anybody can do that. The challenge is to see things from the *other* person's place. What was he thinking? Maybe you were the receiver of fragmentary thought and it didn't come out just right because the beginning and ending weren't there. Or perhaps his ulcer was kicking up, causing him to frown, and you added the frown to the statement he made, giving you a totally erroneous conclusion. You may even not have heard it right! Words are often lost in the crowd at the church door or a room full of chatting people. Check it out; ask for an explanation. Maybe his life is crowded with private suffering you know nothing about. This will color everything he says. If he was laid off his job on Tuesday and things haven't been going too well with his spouse, you may get the angry frustration via a subject totally unrelated. Most criticism is more apropos to the person speaking it than to the person hearing it. Chances are it's *his* problem—and he is trying to live and act normal when nothing is.

So get to know people. Study them. Try to understand their lives. Their routine may be grim indeed—going to work to earn the money to buy the food to get the strength to go to work. A lousy way to live! Your life may be hectic, but it surely isn't dull! But their lives may be, and you ought to know it. Take the opportunity to visit homes whenever possible, preferably in a casual way. This will give you a wealth of knowledge about family interests and has the delightful side effect of reassuring you about your housekeeping. (This technique should not be confused with pastoral calling, which is your husband's job. Feel no obligation to accompany him unless it's your thing or he gives you a special invitation. Remember, he draws the paycheck, not you.)

It helps to understand a person's role in the church also. It goes without saying that you need to know the organizational structure of your church because petty politics sometimes gets involved. People take church offices for all kinds of reasons. *Most* people serve because they love the house of the Lord and are committed to serve him. These people will be your joy, overflowing and abundant. But there are people who take office to *be* somebody. As in any organization, they jealously climb —over you, your husband, or anyone else who happens to be in the way. Recognize them for what they are: people who need help. Understanding their needs takes the sting out of their words and enables you to put them on your prayer list. (You don't have one? Then that's *your* problem . . .)

Befriend those in such need. This will be hard because they will be the most unlovely; but they are most in need of ministry. But never, never become intimate with such people. A good ear and a tight lip are necessities in this and many other personal relationships. The wife who gossips or carelessly spreads around what other people have said only destroys what she values most—her husband.

Do learn to listen. So many people are busy talking in the world that one wonders if *anybody* is listening. The counseling business is thriving—maybe because the only way we can get anyone to listen to us is to pay him! Listening takes time. Good listening takes effort. Productive listening takes understanding. You have to care to listen: care about the problems poured out, care about the hurt, care about the joys. You have to care enough to give your very best . . .

Go heavy on the listening, but cool it with the advice! Stating the problem is often enough to help the person see the obvious solution, especially if the listener wants to understand the whole thing and draws out the background, the little things that have added together to create the problem. When the problem is seen as a unit, the answer sometimes becomes clear.

If you *must* give advice, don't say, "If I were you, I would . . ." You aren't that other person, and he will never be satisfied with your solution, just because it isn't his. On the other hand, if you point out three or four alternative ways to solve the problem, he may grasp at one of them, modify it to meet his inner needs, and be forever grateful that you helped him find an answer. The difference is that the answer is his own—a truly fifth alternative, which would never have worked unless it had come from inside him.

Still tempted to give advice? Consider the fact that few people tell all. They tell what they want you to know, no more. Your information is then faulty, and your advice may be disastrous. On my advice a young wife returned to her husband, only to be cruelly beaten and sexually assaulted. In three hours of sharing she hadn't told me that this kind of treatment was the reason she had left him in the first place. It took a long time for me to forgive myself.

If you feel truly uncertain about listening to people's problems, you can take the easy way and avoid all such possible contacts. Or be adept at saying yes and no, be obviously fidgety, and when they ask, "Am I burdening you?" reply with an anxious, "Well, it *is* getting late . . ."

The fact is, it may be getting late, and you were never meant to be a professional counselor. All these words are *just in case* you must deal with a situation. Your husband is your first referral and should be so always, unless you happen to be a professional counselor and you are *his* first referral. Not many of us fit the professional category, however, so some avoidance techniques are real efficiency tools. You have your own work to do. If you take on the problems of the church people, you will soon find yourself unable to accomplish anything at home. People can easily absorb the time that should be spent with your children, your home, your specialty, your career. So the other side of the coin is to know how to be kind but to remind people firmly that your husband is the minister, not you.

Know your husband's secretary well. She can be your best friend. If he tells you nothing about what's going on, have her keep you informed. Let her know how you feel about being disturbed at home by phone, clue her in when the kids or you are sick, let her be your partner in crime at snatching a private day or two away from the parish. If there is no secretary, learn to take calls well; but after delivering the messages, don't feel personally responsible if he doesn't get all the calls made.

That can lead to nagging and charges of not doing the job. Tell people "about" when your husband will be in, but that you cannot be certain of the time. It is absolutely true that anyone who works with people cannot keep a strict schedule, so always give him plenty of room to wiggle.

If someone starts to pour out a problem suggest that it would really be better if he talked to your husband, since you are not trained to help as he is. If the person persists, you're on. Write down the core of the problem as you hear it and tell the caller you will share it with your husband just as soon as he comes in. The caller may be in crisis: a husband may have just walked out the door forever, a child may have been picked up on drugs, a daughter may have run away. Life for him at that moment has fallen apart. Listening skills are essential then. You are not being the minister, but rather a human who cares when another person bleeds. Someone put it: rejoice with those who rejoice, and weep with those who weep (to paraphrase Paul).

Then, there is the telephone—a subject all by itself. This beautiful emergency device can become an object of extreme hatred. It is the congregation always breaking in on your life, right? Twenty-two phone calls by noon may sound absurd (some of them were), but in some churches it happens. You can't get the washing done, the baby is always wakened, etc. After awhile you are ready to tear the thing out by the roots. Your husband can help you with this one. Let him be the person who suggests to the congregation where and when they should call him. They need to know when he is available anyway. And you need some peace. The plug-in phone, that happy-hour helper, scores here too! When the baby is napping (or you are), you simply unplug the line. You can have dinner undisturbed, or whatever—but do plug it back in!

When your kids get bigger, they can answer the phone, provided you have taught them how to answer it properly. It's worth the effort. Of course, they are bound at some time or other to answer "Dipsy Doodle's Doughnut Den" or "City Morgue." Just pray it doesn't happen when a church dignitary calls . . . the way it did to us.

Getting back to coping with church members in a more specific way, it is of great advantage to have a wide knowledge of various religious doctrines and the behavioral patterns their followers endorse. An Episcopalian and a Baptist just do *not* have the same concept of a minister's wife—or anybody's wife, for that matter. Nor do they have the same concept of each other's Christianity and the actions pursuant to living a Christian life. This makes for a tricky situation if you happen to serve a church in a transient or newly formed area where your church members may be former Presbyterians, Baptists, Lutherans, etc., and a few of your own denomination thrown in to keep everything off—I mean on—balance.

Added to the mix are the liberal and conservative elements of every church, each wanting the church to be like their mode of thought, while you may still be struggling to find peace in the hearts of men and more particularly peace in the heart of your man. Such a conglomerate may substantiate the anti-trust laws: nobody trusts anybody. God forbid that you should find yourself in such a situation; but he hasn't yet, so you had better bone up on who believes what and why.

One of the most difficult situations occurs when dealing with either extreme, liberal or conservative. For what each assumes are equally valid reasons, the liberal will stir up people over social issues that sometimes split a church, while the conservative may pray himself into seclusion from other members because he has the only right way. The truth is that indeed God has spoken to each. One is right, but so is the other. Got that? God speaks to all men in ways they individually understand, but while they may exclude one another from his Grace, he remains completely aloof from such pettiness. He goes right on helping the liberal to change the world's problems and helping the conservative to change men's hearts, managing to work through both. The problem is they are each working from the building diagrams and haven't bothered to look at the master plan.

While they are busy with response to their personal callings, you (or rather your husband) may become the center of what is wrong with the church. If your husband could just speak out on social issues, all would be well; or if he would become involved in speaking in tongues, he could transform the church. Meantime, he is attempting to carry out his own gift of the Spirit: preaching the Word, ministering to the sick and brokenhearted, caring for the unlovely, teaching the babe in Christ. His gift is, of course, hampered by the criticism leveled by both sides, and you find yourself reacting by being overprotecting, or closing yourself off from people, or being tart-tongued, or crying a lot—none of which do any good. In fact, they give your critics more fuel for their fire.

All the answers hardly exist for such a situation, nor do I have omnipotent knowledge (surprised? Well, I still have a lot to say . . .). The only true recourse for you and your husband is, again, openness. To God, to your critics, to each other. Maybe you *do* need to examine your spiritual life—goodness knows, you can lose it in the parsonage as easily as anywhere else! Maybe you aren't taking a stand that needs to be taken. Perhaps you should find out where the two of you are separated in your thinking; you may have been the cause of division unwittingly.

At such a time the level of your love for each other will either rise or fall. Decide to stand together, if you can, to sublimate your individual ideologies so that you become supportive of each other. Bind each other in love, pray for each other, and then love your congregation. Love does turn away wrath.

Do not confuse love, however, with being a doormat. If people accuse you falsely, speak the truth in love, with kindness—not anger. The kinder you become the more angry they appear until they can see themselves as others do. What they do at the moment of self-discovery depends on total forgiveness—as if it never happened at all. Without that they may stalk out of the church angry—forever.

If "Love Thy Neighbor" was the only chapter of this book I had read, I would have divorced my husband before I married him! Up to this point the discussion has aimed at all the difficult things that happen, and that is scarcely fair. Put together, at least fourteen of our sixteen years in the ministry have been good times, with great people. However, you have to survive the two years (that occur in bits and pieces) in order to enjoy the other fourteen, so this chapter has great importance. Instead of scaring you off, though, put it away as ideas for some rough day when you may need to refer to it, and let's talk about the other 90 percent of "church people."

The church is filled with great people, and you don't have to look far to find them. Many of them are by their seeking-for-truth-nature the more introspective, sensitive souls in our world. Some have caught the joy of serving God and put sparkle into each new day. Still others have a depth of faith that inspires and supports you through *any* rough hour. And through all, love abounds. But they *are* people.

People love at all levels, and some are beginners at loving others. Those who have practiced for a lifetime exude warmth and caring. Your problem may be quite different with these great souls—you may have to learn how to receive . . . offers of help, food for your cupboards, babysitting for your children, words of wisdom, respect for your husband, a shoulder to cry on. There is no end to the gifts church people want to give you if you will let them. Most of us, however, have been brought up believing that it is more blessed to give than to receive and have to learn how to accept what people offer. I shall always be grateful to a woman who offered to iron my husband's shirts just after I had undergone surgery. My pride made me say, "Thank you, but it's O.K. I'll manage." She didn't give up, but instead picked up my ironing basket with the words, "You make it awfully hard for the rest of us. If no one will receive, how can the rest of us be blessed for giving?"

So learn to receive with a grateful heart. It makes the other person feel good and helps you learn humility, which all of us could use more of. Since that ironing lesson, I've taken everything offered. Sometimes I know I can't use it, so I simply ask the giver for permission to pass it on to someone else, praising his act of giving. A little extra blessing occurs in receiving; you always have a special feeling for the giver. It warms your heart —and you'll need all the warm heart you can get when the cold days come.

Rule One applies through all these experiences— using your head instead of your emotions. *Decide* to love, even if it hurts or you run the risk of being hurt. *Decide* to be joyful when the house is small and the income smaller. *Decide* to like all the people and to enter into this church to learn and help all you can. *Decide* to rise above the vicissitudes of life, recognizing that trials make you a part of the whole human race. Deciding is setting a mental attitude. In the terms of mind dynamics programs it is a way of programming yourself for joy, or love, or good relationships. Sometimes you even have to decide to love your children or your husband on a day when you feel least loving. Maybe that's what is meant by "be strong in the Lord . . ."

Above all, be yourself—but not your baby self. Be your constantly renewed, growing, mature self, who can enjoy the great people and feel sorrow for the small people. If your self is pleasing to you, you can love that self and, in turn, love your neighbor. If you fail on either of those two statements, then you had better go back to chapter one or ahead to chapter ten. Christ really meant it when he said, "Love thy neighbor as thyself," but loving one's self originates in God. Your self is beautiful because it is a part of all Creation, a creature made in his image and an object of his love. Once you figure that one out, it will be easy to love your neighbor and most of the church members. It will also be possible to understand and then love the rest of the church members who provide the rough places that make you grow. You could even learn to be thankful for them—they are, after all, hastening you on in the race toward perfection! Just don't trip over the Finish Line . . .

6
Parsonage Roulette

Welcome to this chapter, all you lovelies who are lucky enough to live in a house whose exclusive ownership is of the church, by the church, and for the church . . . and is overseen with exquisite care by a parsonage committee that either never quits or never starts. Granted, this kind of parsonage is literally falling from the scene, but, until the last porch collapses, someone is *bound* to live in the house.

The key to success in the parsonage system is to remember the motto that somebody must have said sometime: "Always turn problems into possibilities!" You might try rehearsing those last three words in your mind as a defense against your next assignment . . . problems into possibilities, problems into possibilities.

Come with me on a tour of my first parsonage home, which is still in use today, some sixteen years later. It was over a hundred years old when we approached the steps, and had once served as the church sanctuary. When a fine church was built some fifty years later, the old building was carefully moved down the hill and across the street to nestle in a grove of huge shade trees. It was divided into two stories, rooms were partitioned off, and a coal-burning furnace, very necessary for a New Jersey winter, placed in the basement. Newly refurbished, the house must have seemed quite elegant to its first residents, offering a complete study for the pastor, a large living room, dining room, and kitchen on the first floor, with two large bedrooms, sewing room, and bath on the second. Some years later someone decided that the kitchen needed updating, so linoleum wall covering had been placed on the walls, and handsome cupboards and a large sink made a dream workspot. Got the picture? A really nice, comfortable house . . .

Now, are you ready to go in the door with me?

Fifty more years have gone by. The first thing you notice is the furniture. Then the wallpaper. Next, the worn linoleum on the dining room floor. And the kitchen wallboard all unglued and fanning gently when the wind blows. And the separation between the wall and the door leading to the basement. And the church people coming to the door on Sunday morning to ask if they may use your bathroom (when your son is in there brushing his teeth in the nude).

Then you notice that the church is quite a way from you on one side, there is nothing but trees on the other side, you don't know anyone in town, the telephone is downstairs, and your husband is leaving at 5:00 A.M. Tuesday for seminary and won't be back till Friday, and you're alone in a town with no police force!

That night you notice a whole slew of new things. The house creaks and groans in the night. Somewhere a cat howls, and you are sure that a baby has fallen down the old well hole in the backyard. The trees whistle, which sets you wondering what you would do if a hurricane came through like those the people have been telling you about. Then, the house begins to get cold, so you worry about your child, but by this time it takes all the courage you have to get up to see that he is covered.

Gradually, you realize that the thermostat isn't working because probably the coal fire has gone out—and you never built one in your life . . .

So developed the Parsonage Canon: (a) Get acquainted with your house. Know its flaws and good points well, listen to its creaks, soak up the atmosphere of the house —all before you pass judgment. You may discover that the house that creaks the most lives the best. Then apply (b) Live awhile. Now, if perchance you have a committee that only decorates when pastors move in, you will have to cram a lot of living into thirty-six hours or less and let your mind go on a life-spree.

Who goes where is probably the first question to settle. Be selfish. Start by deciding which room will be yours and then divide up the rest of the space by any of a hundred facts: who's youngest, who fights the most, who is the best housekeeper (he goes closest to the front door), who's the noisiest, who's the biggest eavesdropper (no open vent in *that* room) . . .

Once this major decision is out of the way it is time to move on to each person's life-style. If there is a drummer in the house, he gets the back room, no matter what. After all, as long as he has his drums and his bed, he probably won't notice anything else. Or maybe you have a clay addict—you know, always sculpting (alias messing)—then, no rug for that room. Forget the wall paper for the one with the poster collection— or go mod and paper the walls with the posters . . .

Oh! Don't forget the dirty clothes. Without a Central Collecting Agency or a Night Deposit Box, you're doomed. This problem alone could determine where everyone is situated. If your husband can't seem to walk to the clothes hamper from the bedroom, then you have just three choices: (1) a hamper in every bedroom and bathroom, (2) putting the most slovenly the closest to the collection point, or (3) constantly being a pickup (which is really not too appropriate for a minister's wife). There is a fourth alternative, of course, but most congregations balk at the cost of installing pneumatic clothes chutes from every room.

Now that the big questions are settled you can quickly work through the simpler task of selecting paint and/or paper. If you go for the latter, find out who gets to put the paper on the wall *before* you buy. Ministers have a tendency to lose their religion while wallpapering and some wives have been known to neglect their families in a fanatical drive to "finally get this house done!" Neither condition is easily understood by the church member who drops in to see how things are coming, especially if the dirty clothes situation has not been solved and your eavesdropper happens to quote what Father said just a few minutes ago.

But if you do decide for paper, let yourself enjoy a positive attitude (otherwise translated as "I'm the one who has to live with it, not the committee"). Many a dreary parsonage dots the land because the minister's wife was afraid to say what she thought or state what she wanted. After all, she scarcely knows the people she is working with, they *are* telling her all the terrible choices of days gone by, the chairman is constantly reminding her that this is a parsonage and we must stay with neutrals so the next woman can live with it. The falsity of her reasoning is obvious at that point—how many neutral ministers' wives do you know?

So let yourself go. Dare to say those magic words: "I really like this" or their companion piece, "No; that doesn't quite suit our family life-style." Be sure to avoid phrases like "I think purple is just horrible" or "Flowered wallpaper turns my stomach!" After all, the chairman may have her house done completely in purple flowers and have a tendency to turn the same livid color . . .

So choose what you live with well. If you are not gifted with decorating skills, seek advice from someone whose home you admire and feel comfortable in or from a professional decorator. If neither is available, use the old rule of thumb (it will be old by the time this book is published) and surround yourself with the colors you most like to wear. Any woman looks best in a house that suits her natural coloring and personality, so if the paint company charts look like an impenetrable maze, go look in your closet to see what color predominates and figure out which of your outfits makes you feel happiest. Your accessories will give you clues to accent colors, but, if you are poor like the rest of us and always stick to basic black and brown, then go to the closest Sears' or Ward's catalogs and pick out the accessories you would buy if you could. Then, translate all this knowledge about wardrobe and color into shades of the same combinations, remembering to mute the big blocks of color and splash the accents in bright shades.

Letting the children select their own color combinations is not only good for them (it gives them a sense of belonging), but helps the committee understand the necessity of making the parsonage a home for each pastor and his family and gets the problem off your back. It is, after all, the only home your family will remember, so as much as possible it ought to be theirs. If their choice is black and white swirls that make you dizzy, you simply tell people your children picked it out. The adults will give you a knowing look that says they understand the problem, and the kids will think you are really terrific and wish their parents would let them do the same.

By now, you may be feeling slightly extravagant. Not because you have spent any more, mind you, but just because you feel as if this is really your house. Relax. With every stroke of the paint roller just remind yourself that if the next wife doesn't like it, she can paint over it just the way you're doing. Or you can consider the educational value of helping the church to see the need of decorating for a new family just as a renter would do for a new tenant. If that reasoning fails, face the truth that when the home is aesthetically satisfying to you and your husband, he will come home to a happier wife and place, be a happier man, and a more able pastor and preacher. It is much easier for a man to cope with heavy burdens in his job if his home is a soothing oasis. So paint away and enjoy.

Speaking of heavy burdens, there is also the problem of furniture. Enlarged it includes moving bills, too much for too small a house, too little for too large a house, "Early Family" in an elegant neighborhood, none at all, etc. Some churches own all or most; others may have only curtains and refrigerator. Fortunately, many conferences, synods, or what not have thought about this and attempted to bring some uniformity to their areas. Some of your difficulty will be solved by knowing what is expected in your location. One area we served provided everything, even the pots in the cupboard. So, of course, we bought nothing. Then, came the time of moving to another state, and we found ourselves with a parsonage that was empty but supposed to be full. The church was poor and so were we, so they bought half and we bought half—sort of. Our half is still with us—sort of.

The problem is more likely to be with what the church has than what it does not have. When you move into a house and the chairs have the stuffing falling out of the arms, it tends to discourage you, especially if the chairs have just been cleaned in preparation for your coming. Fortunately, slipcovers work miracles. So does a course at the local high school in upholstery. If that is not your thing, then appeal to your committee. Maybe the problem is lack of funds in the budget—then work to put a furniture item in next year's budget. It should never be left out, even if never spent, and at least a portion ought to be cumulative to replace major items when they wear out.

When you buy, don't do as we did! Buy the very best you can afford, because chances are it will follow you for many years. Then again, if you can't afford much, check those want ads daily. It takes time but yields high quality for low cost. Paint and patience are your most valuable allies in the furniture department. You can color-coordinate for very little money and take pride in the results besides.

Experiment with arrangement. Few committees are left that tell you what room what furniture may reside in. (Should you meet up with one, throw a furniture-arranging party and let them help in the fun of undoing what they think is perfect. Their new product will also be perfect.) New arrangements of furniture often transform a room, and even the poorest furniture can take on a new look by having a different background. Leave a light on for your husband at night, though. You wouldn't want him to break a leg in the dark.

If your house simply lacks minor things that you don't have but that would be an asset to the church property, invite the women's society in for coffee and goodies. Once they are fed, invite them to tour the house on their own, but tell them they will find little notes around the house that will give them an opportunity to make their parsonage lovelier. All they need do is sign their name to the slip and you will know (and so will all the other ladies!) they have pledged to make that spot their contribution. Minimal preparation is needed for this tour. The house should be clean, of course. Then notes prepared that read, "Wouldn't a pair of boudoir lamps be nice here?" or "A mirror to check your hat as you go out the door would be such a help in this spot!" Once they catch on, signing their names becomes a status thing and they join in the game eagerly. They feel good, and so do you.

There is a possibility that a much larger problem may confront you. *Your family may not fit.* Too many people and too little house. If this is true, you must move cautiously and with great tact. The facts will be obvious from the beginning, and the first responsibility lies with the person who sent you there if you are under an appointive system. Refer to him for help. If you accepted a call to this church, then you may need even greater discretion for there is no easy solution. The options? Add onto the present house, buy a new house and sell the traditional residence of all the ministers for years and years (a tough one!), rent the parsonage and have the church give you a rental allowance so you may find your own more spacious quarters (with more spacious amounts of money to come from your own pocket), put birth control pills in the church budget, or send a couple of the kids to live with your mother. Not recommended, but possible as a last resort, is for *you* and the kids to go live with your mother, accompanied by an announcement in the church paper that you have done so while awaiting some solution to the problem of fitting your family into the parsonage and that you hope to be reunited with your husband soon!

If in fact, you alone must make the congregation aware of the size of the house in relation to your needs, the best way to do this is to move everything in as if it would fit, and then invite people in. Don't move a thing! If the baby's bed is crammed in between the couch and chair in the living room, leave it there. Just be sure to have the baby cross and grouchy that day so he does not entertain everyone . . . By no means apologize for people having to step over things or for jamming them into small areas. Let it happen. However, see that your parsonage committee is there to assist with refreshments or something so that they, too, experience the crowd scene.

An alternate solution is to use the study (if there is one) for a bedroom and find space at the church for an office (if there isn't one). Churches are usually more aware of a minister's working needs than his family's needs and, therefore, more willing to assist. If it appears that this is the best solution, do it completely. What you are suffering in lack of space has probably been the bane of every family's existence in that house, so correct it (unless, of course, you have no self-restraint and nine kids). Make the bedroom permanently a bedroom. A half-done or temporary correction on a parsonage is rarely finished or temporary.

If your choice is to add onto the present house, stumble over one another for awhile so that you and the trustees can plan carefully and well. Survey the neighborhood to see if you would be overbuilding. If you are, then settle the question of whether this house is always (meaning twenty years or so) to be the parsonage. If the answer is yes, then overbuild with confidence. However, not without guidelines. Your conference or presbytery probably has some committee that concerns itself with housing. Get its recommendations regarding size and so forth, and make sure every person involved in the planning has a copy and reads it. Refer to it in every meeting. That way they are not basing actions on your desires but are bringing their parsonage up to preset standards. It helps quiet the critics, too.

Hire an architect if you can; but if not, find a contractor with a solid reputation in home additions who is willing to work with the committee the way an architect would. His services should be paid separate from the bid on the expansion so that his planning has no strings attached.

Adding on is messy and inconvenient but well worth it if the end product results in happier living and a pleased congregation. Be cheerful about the mess. Figure the extra holes in the wall make it easier to call the kids. Plan to take a short vacation during part of the work—short unless someone is appointed specifically to check the work every day so that plans are adhered to. Get the people involved in it where possible—painting, cleaning up, furniture moving, whatever. Let it be exciting for them to see it happen. After all, how many ministers get to live in a holy house?

Should buying a newer house be the decision of the church officers, for goodness' sake (and yours too), let them carry the ball. Let them present it to the congregation, let them do the searching, let them do the financing —but you do the guiding. Know your church housing standards. Know what the needs of a parsonage are over against the needs of a regular house. Know the level of housing of your congregation and try not to exceed it. Stay clear of buying a showcase house. What you need is adequacy, both in aesthetics and in space. And when tempted by an enormous, beautiful house, just remember who has to keep it clean!

The final decision must be that of the church officials and the congregation. If it is yours and the house is later discovered to be a poor purchase, you will be to blame for eons. Don't hesitate, however, to make a choice between two or three houses, or to veto a house that you honestly feel would be inadequate. Parsonages need to fit not only family needs but entertaining needs as well. You may not like to entertain, but the next wife may find it her joy. Purchasing is the time when you *must* think of all the families that might live there, not just your own likes and dislikes. Leave that to decorating.

A rental allowance is a modern solution to housing needs and often results in the church leaving the landlord business and the minister securing a home like any other person—out of his salary (even if they call it "rental allowance"). If your church is accustomed to long pastorates, this may be the right choice. You are then removed from parsonage roulette. Instead, you belong to the homeowner, taxpayer group and have much greater understanding of the problems of your members. When taxes go up, usable income goes down. You are more aware of the power of your vote. If your child kicks the wall in or breaks a window, no committee comes rushing to your aid to replace it. Nor is there the possibility of discounted prices often accorded to churches for purchases. In addition, if the phone should ring and the "Voice" says you are to be moved, there is no company to take over your house or much grace time to sell. If property isn't moving in your area, you may have a house standing empty for a long time with payments coming due with painful regularity.

On the other hand, if the house is yours, you can do as you please with no one to say otherwise. Your sculptor can drop clay, the posters can go up, the drums bang away, you can entertain or not with no sense of obligation either way—in short, you can have the experience of a personal home and the responsibility.

Renting may be a good solution if you are able to find a house in your church locale. This is not always possible, and availability should be a major consideration before a church decides to take this step. Also, if the parsonage is rented out in order to give you a rental allowance for a larger home, very clear lines should be drawn about the use of church furniture or equipment that may be in the parsonage. If it is left in the parsonage, then you may be running a heavy deficit for furniture purchase or rental of a furnished home.

The question of the effects of non-permanency upon the family must be considered, whatever the solution. Many families move two or three times during their lifetime in the United States today, but a minister's family knows that it will move perhaps every four to seven years—forever. There are exceptions, of course, but moving is always there in the mind of each family member. Will these people be my friends next year? Do I dare make friends? If I do, will I suddenly have to leave them? Renting may add to this omnipresent awareness of impermanence!

So what to do? Arm yourself with a decorating course or two, take a positive attitude, learn to look for the good in every house, and learn to love the houses you live in. Every house wants to be a home, but only you can make it one by your attitude and efforts. It takes courage to love a parsonage, work with a committee, and satisfy your family needs. But it is worth the effort! The home you live in now will be the one your family's memories are stored in tomorrow. So go ahead—dare to take the initiative. And remember, nothing improves a house as much as a loved-in-look.

7
Everybody Shift

Nicely settled? Well . . .

You've known for weeks now, but somehow you still aren't prepared. You heard the announcement—you've been assigned to a new church. Your stomach knots, and you clutch your husband's hand tightly. Till this moment you just had not realized how settled you were in this house, this community, this church, and now the order is to leave it all—forever. This chapter of your life is finished. What you haven't accomplished you never will. You've had your chance . . .

And the committee from the new church wants to meet you. Quick, comb your hair, brush off your husband's shoulders, pull up your slip strap, and look fantastic. Remember, those first impressions can be last ones! Perk up your smile and get the wetness out of your eyes—look expectant (I always was), full of excitement. There they are! Amazing how nice they are to you, considering they didn't want their pastor to leave; they really talked very little about him. Those questions about the children and the pets got a little personal, and you don't think they approved of your question about their minister's wife working. You had to ask it, though, to be honest. That one man on the committee almost got to your husband, wanting to know what kinds of texts he used and how often he preached on social issues—even warning that folks in their church didn't go for any of this "guitar-playing folk stuff" in the worship service. To think that just an hour ago you were worried about leaving and now you feel apprehensive about going! If you happen to be a drinking woman, you had better swear off right now because the next three weeks could turn you into a real lush!

Moving—parsonage style—is scarcely done the way your parishioners do it. For them it is probably a decision made over many months of planning and conversation. Or, if their company makes the decision, it may be more abrupt but a whole lot easier physically. Companies usually pay for packing and moving so that they just live normally right up to the day of leaving. The movers come in, and the family walks out. (Granted, the garbage may be packed, but that is a small price to pay for the convenience.)

No such luck for you unless you happen to have a connection at Fort Knox. A few quick calls convince you that scavenging boxes behind the local markets might be in order, and you send the kids all over the neighborhood collecting newspapers to wrap your best china in. Carefully, you empty the cupboards one by one, assured that *this* time everything will be marked and nothing lost. No more of those last-minute collection boxes marked "miscellaneous"—it takes years to sort all that stuff! By noon your back is beginning to ache and you are cursing materialism. Five years ago you didn't have half this much. Where did it come from? And you haven't left the kitchen yet. Your mind flies off to the electric guitars and drums in the bedroom, quickly inventories the yard goods in the sewing cupboard, the tools in the garage. Urgency creeps into your voice as you send out for another load of boxes.

The phone rings. This isn't the first time, of course, more like the twenty-first. People are sorry to hear the news and can they help? Squelch that pride—say "Yes" . . . but only to a chosen few who love you and will understand that when you move, all the dust of the earth suddenly appears behind beds and chairs, under boxes, in the drapes. Pick the helpers who will clean the oven and know that their own is dirty. Criticism is not what you need right now!

The clock moves on, and so do you. When *will* your husband come home? What on earth is he doing at the church all this time? Doesn't he know his work is finished at this place and he should just shut down? Like a lightning bolt it hits you: his office! Books from floor to ceiling on all four walls. He must have a ton of books. Still disgruntled, you forgive your earlier thoughts as you realize the packing *he* must be doing.

A young son moves through the maze that is growing in the middle of the house, trailed by several friends. You open your mouth to tell them not to touch anything and are startled to hear yourself screaming at these innocent children! You grab a wet towel and a cup of coffee, clear off your favorite chair, put up your feet, and plop the towel across your forehead. You must get calm! You're only moving, and you have to set a good example for the children. Something crashes in the kitchen . . . suddenly, you remember the crystal vase you left sitting on the counter, an heirloom from your grandmother. Desperately, you pull the towel over your face and squall like a baby . . .

Somehow, sometime, you manage to pull yourself

back together, and the packing continues, punctuated by invitations to dinner from all the people who have meant to have you in all during your pastorate there. As long as they let you come in your grubbies, these meals are like manna in the wilderness (which is what the house is beginning to look like!). You are aware you are falling a little behind your original timetable, but if you work very hard, you can still be ready when the van comes on Tuesday. The new family is moving into the house on Wednesday afternoon, and the church has cleaners coming in Tuesday afternoon. It is going to be nip and tuck! The problem is leaving Sunday clothes out, keeping enough kitchen supplies to fix what meals you have to, sorting what to take and what to throw out or give away, keeping the beds intact with all their linens . . . The budget ruled out a motel for the last night, especially since you found out that your husband doesn't have a ton of books, he has a ton and a half! You are faced with the rising cost of moving, over and above anything the church will pay. Oh, well, no vacation this year! And Sunday is the Farewell Tea.

Sunday morning dawns with radiant sunshine. One glance in the mirror, and you know you'll never match it. If only your makeup wasn't packed, you could cover the bags under your eyes. Maybe if you squint a lot, nobody will notice. A call for help from the bedroom; somehow your husband's shoes have disappeared. Quick recall tells you that the woman who helped you yesterday probably packed them—but in which box? You scan the writing on each one—nothing reads "front bedroom" or "master bedroom." How did she mark that box? Frantically, you start tearing open boxes you think might be right, and in the fifth one you find the shoes—

at the very bottom of the box. Before the whole family is dressed, you have opened four more cartons and you are very late. What happened to your careful planning? No matter now. You stash the kids in the car and head for church. It isn't till they are getting out that you realize your youngest has on one green sock and one red. You tell him to keep his pants legs down, take a deep breath, and hurry into the church building.

If your welcome party was called a reception, this bon voyage tea ought to be called a "deception." You're supposed to look lovely (you're barely holding together), people say a lot of nice things (most of which you don't deserve), they give you a gift (which you have no idea how you're going to pack), everybody cries (probably because the gift cost so much), and your husband makes a speech about what this church has meant to him (too much to say) and what the next one will be like (of which he knows nothing). Then, they may ask you to tell them about the new parsonage, which you've seen once, or to sing a song in an exhausted voice. Meantime, the children are putting in their two cents' worth whenever they can, thoroughly enjoying the limelight, and totally aware that this is one time they can get away with it. You don't know whether to laugh or cry, since you may actually be glad you're leaving—or you may be sorry to leave but so excited about the new place that you are having difficulty concealing it. Such an emotional flood will make a new highwater mark every time you move. You might just as well learn to swim in it.

Let's backpaddle a bit. How come you're moving anyway? If you are under the appointive system as we are, you probably went through a conference with a committee recommending whether you were to stay or go. Before that, however, you might have had a call from the top man in your area sounding you out about whether you *wanted* to stay or go. Maybe you just sense that your major work at this place is done; perhaps the whole pastorate has been stormy; maybe your family is hurting in this particular place—whatever the case, your inner self has been telling you it's time to move. (If you initiate the move, you can expect to have trouble feeling sad about leaving!) Under the call system, your husband may have received a call to try out for another pastorate, and you have seen committees, visited the church, and *you* decided whether or not to take the offer. And, of course, in either system there is always the possibility that your church has asked you to leave. Ouch!

It hurts to be weighed in the balance and be found wanting. Always take a good look at the scales in such a case. What was your husband's work measured on? Was the decision a just one or a ruse to get rid of a man they didn't agree with? There is the possibility that you were mis-sent—you would never have fit in with this community because you are truly dissimilar from the people who live there. This is the time for real soul-searching—but keep it honest. Don't lick your wounds and surrender to self-pity. Take a good hard look at what you do and how you do it so that you can learn from your mistakes. If you are asked to move often, then it is time for the question, Do we belong in the ministry? (See chapter twelve.)

We shall suppose that you are leaving under happy circumstances (as happy as you can muster when you are tearing your life up by the roots), you know you are going to move, and you have to tell somebody or burst! Resist that impulse to tell your best friend first—unless, of course, she lives in Someplace Else and will be struck dumb by the news. Start with somebody official —the board, the pastoral relations committee, the head deacon—somebody in office. Let him take it from there. Of course, you may enjoy surprises and so you tell no one until appointments are announced in the morning paper. This may bring many cries of outrage upon your superiors in case you have something against them, but it scarcely helps the man who will follow you. And if you have been well liked, he'll need your help. The practical joker among us may choose to line the study with moving boxes and start emptying his bookshelves, or simply disappear one morning never to return. These methods are not recommended except in desperate situations (like you know the house will be bombed at sundown).

About that man who is to follow you—your husband will have the task of acquainting him with the church and its people vicariously, but you can do a very helpful thing for his family. Make a list of names of the doctor, dentist, grocery store, service stations, and other local information. Have a parsonage folder with all the instructions and guarantees for equipment that belongs in the house, a list of wall paint colors (leave leftover paint marked in the garage if you have any), and leave the place CLEAN. Well do I remember a parsonage with a basement full of rotting pumpkins. I remember the smell, the mess, and the family who left them . . . When the van leaves, either I stay behind or somebody I've hired to polish and sweep—and more than once I have turned around and started cleaning all over again at the next place. If cleanliness is next to godliness, we wives are going to have to work harder or we won't make it into heaven!

So you pick up your brooms and brushes, do a last Carol Burnett act in the kitchen, and say a final farewell to your house. Try walking through a clean, empty house, pausing in each room to remember all that happened there—the powder dumped all over the dresser and floor by a two-year-old, the child who fought for his life in that bed by the windows, the picture of a daughter on a special date coming down those stairs— and then quietly say goodbye to each room, closing the doors behind you. The wallpaper and paint are yours, the slipcovers sprang from your sewing machine, the table refurbished to serve again was your pride and joy. So you touch, remember, and set this house forever in your mind. I have even been known to speak aloud to the house as I closed the door for the last time . . . something like words of appreciation for warmth and shelter. Sentiment? Not really. It somehow helps to close the pages on that part of your life so that you are ready for the new; as someone said, "You have to pull down a mental windowshade so you don't keep looking back" (even if your husband's name isn't Lot!).

And now for the new—church, house, neighbors, friends, playmates. The cat carrier is stashed on the floor between your feet, a prized but fragile possession rides gingerly on your lap, and your body sinks gratefully into the cushioned seat—that is, if you have only one car. If there are two, you may find yourself driving a car loaded to the roof with all the leftovers—those miscellaneous items you weren't going to have this time. You not only still have them but you ran out of boxes, and they aren't even packed! How can someone so well organized get herself into such a mess? The driving is a good feeling even if you are tired. It gives you time to think, to refocus your brain, to start planning and dreaming about your destination. You try to remember the floor plan of the house and put the furniture into each room. Which painting should go over the fireplace? When the pictures go up, you feel as though you're home, so that should be done early. You kick yourself for buying a batch of new towels in the January sales— all matched to your *last* house. That's a problem for later.

The scenery around you begins to change, sharpening the realization that you really are going to live in a new place. You note that the driving distance is just right—far enough away that people won't come often to see you, but close enough to share an occasional lunch with your best friend . . . your eye catches the name of a restaurant that might be a good trysting place. And so it goes until you see those first signs announcing your new address. You feel your nerves tense a little with anticipation as your eyes scramble for position to see all they can. Everything is suddenly important: grocery stores, schools, the way people keep their houses, the condition of the streets—each thing tells you about the town you are about to call home. Then you make that crucial turn. Three blocks more, turn right, and it's the fifth house on the left-hand side. The speed of the car drops till you are almost crawling when you arrive at the driveway. There it is—waiting for your touch. You've done it! You are officially moved. Out, that is.

A group of smiling ladies stands on the porch waiting to help you move in. You are a mess. And if they help you unpack, you won't have any secrets from any-body . . . You swallow the threat in your throat and climb out of the car, get caught in a windfall of names, and go through the door for the grand tour, directed by the president of the women's society (or is she the parsonage committee chairman?). Before you can size up the situation and get acquainted, someone announces that the van has arrived and the men want to know where everything goes. If only you knew!

Several hours and a thousand answers later you crawl into a sleeping bag (where *did* you put those sheets and blankets?) and huddle close to your equally exhausted husband. The bed feels lumpy (the grooves don't fit), you haven't figured out how to make the furnace work, and there's no milk for breakfast. Your husband is the only familiar landmark in the whole scene, but since he is sharing your bed, you guess you must be in the right house after all!

The next few days are full of questions, mostly beginning with "where is?" or "did you find?" Carton by carton you reverse the procedure of the last three weeks. Cupboards are lined and filled, boxes tossed out back, pictures hung (finally), old things rediscovered. Neighbors make themselves known, church members bring in food for your table (bless them!), you are investigated by the children on the block, and tentative friendships are begun. You are aware from time to time that your emotions have yet to catch up, but these times become less frequent as you actually begin to know where to find the salad dressing at the market and there are ten families you can identify by name. The new address becomes familiar (especially after all those change-of-address forms you sent out), and the house begins to feel like home. It will still take a while. There are the schools to investigate, you have yet to find the best place to shop (who's had time to do any?), but that will happen a day at a time. The best part is that you survived the crisis, even the welcome reception. You have moved out —and in.

About this time you may feel overwhelmed with an urge to settle someplace in a home of your own. Reject it immediately. It is the work of the Devil! Even if it isn't, think of all the experiences you would have missed, the new people you would never have met, the community you would never have shared. One thing about it: life in the parsonage is seldom dull and sometimes so exciting you can scarcely live through it! Take your bows—you are an amazing woman!

8
The Hostess
with the Leastest

Now, my dear, you have five hundred new people out there somewhere just waiting to meet you—and your marvelous family! You only *thought* there were five thousand last Sunday, when, actually, the figure is quite manageable. You simply take five hundred and divide it by the weeks in the year and entertain nine and a half people each week. Never mind that you have church functions, scout meetings, choir practice, college one night a week—this is the answer to your problem. In one short year you will have entertained every single person in your home, even added new members as they joined, and everyone will think you are fantastic—the Perle Mesta of the Parsonage Set.

Granted, you may quickly begin to feel more like a pooped pearl wishing you could just hide in your oyster, but you will have included every single soul. This remarkable feat will be remembered forever since you are the *only* minister's wife who ever accomplished it. It will go a long way toward hushing the tongues that suggest the minister's family is looking positively poor these days and it does seem that if he can afford to entertain so much he ought to keep his family looking better. Some people are just never satisfied!

Entertaining is an art (it must be if I'm so klutzy at it). Art is a natural endowment that can be cultivated by great teachers, exploded upon the world by infatuated devotees, and heralded by princes and powers as history itself. The art of entertaining simply begins in the galley instead of the gallery and ends in the disposal—either human or mechanical, depending on its success. In between are the sub-arts of conversation, conviviality, table design, people mixing, and "calamity awaral." (Don't look in the dictionary—it's not there.) Of all the sub-arts that make up your great gift, the last is the one you will do best to develop astutely. Calamity visits when least expected and, therefore, you must always stay alert to her coming.

For example, it was the first dinner attempted by a young minister's wife. Candles were lit, all was in place but the few last dishes of food, the guests were arriving in good spirits. Our hostess, however, was falling slightly behind schedule and hurrying faster—always a disastrous solution. As the dinner hour approached, she gave her husband the sign to call the guests just as soon as she put on the salad bowl. Naturally, he failed to hear the end of the sentence so her guests poured into the dining area; whereupon, she grabbed the salad, putting it down so fast that it never stopped moving—until it hit the wall, tipped over the edge of the table and scattered its contents decoratively upon the waiting floor . . . and tablecloth . . . and wallpaper. Such courage! Such fortitude! She broke the heavy silence by saying, "Well, I guess we won't have salad for dinner. Let's begin anyway." And without so much as glancing at the salad bowl now resting innocently at her feet, she picked up a plate and handed it to the first guest, laughing all the while at her own clumsiness. Now, this may be modern art instead of traditional, but the dinner was not ruined by the presence of calamity; by the time the evening was over, it had become the high point of the humor shared among the guests. What an artist!

Someday women's magazine editors are going to have to answer for what they have done to you and me, making us think that the only way to entertain is to be perfect. The house must be spotless, the china should gleam, the food be beautiful as well as delectable, the recipes secret, and the hostess must always remain with her guests—servants or no. If there is a curse on the women of America, this is it! How do you serve and sit down at the same time, anyway? And what if all you know how to make is baked potatoes and meat loaf? Or what if the only china you have is plastic from the nearest discount house and your cups are strictly mix and matchless? What do you do then? Hide in the closet?

Oh, the agony of soul I have endured over such traumatic questions. Never shall I forget the shredded potatoes that turned black because no one told me to keep them covered with water while I was working with them. Thank God for cheese—it covers a multitude of sins! If only, long ago, someone had explained to me that entertaining was about the people who came, not the person receiving them. Of course, sometimes they keep coming . . . and coming . . . and coming . . . so that the food meant for ten must be tithed many times to feed the multitude.

Entertaining may not be your thing, but inevitably somebody in the family is bound to invite someone in. Perhaps a well-meaning churchman will tell you how beautifully the former minister's wife entertained, implying, of course, that you have lived in the parsonage for two years and when are you ever going to have people in? Your gift may be professional tennis or boxing —can't anyone understand how incompatible entertaining is with athletics? You even get to feeling that after all it *is* your home and you can do as you please. And you will be exactly right. The idea that you must entertain is a leftover (and who serves leftovers?) from ages happily past when you were the church hostess and unofficial pray-er. In those days if you could do those two things well (plus keep your children in line, be an immaculate housekeeper, dress perfectly, etc.), not much else mattered. That concept of you we must assume is now passé—and even if it isn't, assume it anyway. You'll be much happier.

This simple assumption frees you to use the parsonage as you would your own home—which it is supposed to be, not a church living room. Granted your husband is in public relations; any public relations man entertains slightly more than the mail clerk, so you do have some responsibility to *him* (not the church) as an assist in his work. The question is how much, or when, or how? And on what? Close behind these questions comes the idea of the home as a place in which the family lives and what rights they have. Aren't they due some privacy?

With all these things to consider, you can quickly see that entertaining for you is slightly more than picking out a recipe and planning a menu. Thousands of books have been written to help you in that department. *Your* problems are unique. To wit, perhaps your husband has been assigned to a brand-new church—to form it, in fact—and your house is the only meeting place available except the school used for Sunday services. This could well mean that for awhile there is a group using your living room four nights a week. In addition, your husband's study is in the house, so callers are coming constantly (if he's doing a good job, that is). No book on hostessing covers how to do the wash, discipline the kids, get through the measles, mumps, and chicken pox, take a bath, prepare three meals a day, scrub the kitchen floor and make the beds, all while being radiantly lovely.

Or maybe it isn't a new church, but merely a parsonage located between the church and the parking lot the way one of ours was. On hot summer days people would drive into the lot and call to us through the open windows as we sat at meals (or changed clothes in the bedroom which was on the church side). They would knock at the door to make sure the minister was not there before they took the trouble to go the twenty-five more yards to the church office, then cut through the backyard as they left, leaving the gate open and our small children unprotected. I counted ten weeks in a row when someone came to the door while I was trying to wash my hair! TV commercials notwithstanding, I never have looked like a delectable hostess with suds dripping off the end of my nose.

Such experiences tend to make one fight for privacy, to say the least. You might even be heard to wish that everybody would just go away and leave you alone! Justified. All humans have to have quiet time. Your need is the reverse of the entertaining manuals—not how to have people in, but how to keep them out till you want them to come in. In fairness to the people, however, remember that each person thinks he is the only one who comes to your door—after all, he sees no one else there but you and the children. Even the arrival of another person as he is leaving will be thought a coincidence, not a normal occurrence. Hating them or the church for not seeing your condition is useless. Action is needed—kind, constructive action coupled with clear communication.

And the first person you must communicate with is your husband. You can throw a picket line in front of the door, or stand up in church at witness time and witness to what is *really* going on in your life, but the results would probably be rather drastic. (Maybe you wouldn't have to live there at all!) Better to explain carefully that you must have his help in crowd control; would he please speak to the congregation about the problem, or put a notice in the church paper, or disconnect the telephone and the doorbell, or get a new wife because you are stark-raving mad and can't stand another minute of it! When you have quit screaming, he may understand . . .

It is possible that part of the problem is your husband —*he* is the one who never sees the condition of the house, who invites people in even if they've come only to drop off a list of names (and are actually in a hurry), or who calls meetings for the house instead of the church because he likes the informal atmosphere. And you may have assisted him in developing this attitude when you served that first fateful dessert and coffee to the committee gathered in your home. That was the hostess-thing to do and you were innocent. A woman I know literally destroyed herself in the kitchen. She was the original "bake and shake." Her recipes were famous, her serving impeccable, but the heavy doses of tranquilizers were scarcely the end product she had meant to achieve. All the while her husband thought it was something she loved to do . . .

Desserts are in order—sometimes. Meetings are in order—sometimes. But don't be selfish. Let others have the pleasure of people in *their* homes; or if their houses aren't big enough, let them share the honors of being your hostess for the evening. You might even develop a corps of parsonage hostesses who take turns throughout the year so that you are free to meet people or to be away to carry on a normal life for yourself without hurting the development of the church life. Volunteers are usually easy to find since hostessing at somebody else's house is always fun because they don't have to clean and are given access to another woman's inner sanctum: her kitchen and best china. Besides, they get to be "in" on all that's happening. These women can also become your very close friends.

This crowd- and husband-control process should not be expected to happen overnight. It is a gradual education of attitudes. Meanwhile, how are yours? Get a firm grip on yourself so you can honestly face how you feel about people. Are you afraid to have them come in because you can't stand the exposure? Is there a critic at the door every time the bell chimes? If your answers to those two questions are in the affirmative, then it's time to set up some personal privacy limits. For some weird reason, taking a shower and washing my hair were always things I needed privacy for. What then was I to do when the doorbell rang? With the car parked outside it was obvious that someone was home; so after the bell went unanswered, a loud knocking ensued, and the more persistent then came to the back door. The answer was so simple—but for me it took a trip to the hospital and a doctor to point it out. Put a note on the door asking people to please go to the church office for church business. To my amazement people not only did so during my illness but continued to do so afterward because they had become accustomed to it. The doorbell rang less and less until I actually began to look forward to someone coming to the door because I knew she was coming to see me as a friend. That was neat!

If the office is in the house, you may need to post some hours or set up a message box, complete with a note that the minister is out calling or whatever. Be honest, though, and include a note saying he is at home when he is. And since the telephone can tear your privacy apart as much as the doorbell, an investment in a phone answering service or recorder may well save your mental health (and your marriage!).

Please note: so far we have been dealing with the extreme—not the parsonage that is four miles away but the one next door or the one that serves as the church. When you live farther away, much of this tension relaxes. The trouble is that you have no guarantee that Next Door will never happen to you! If the scouts can be prepared, so can we!

You are not the sole reason for all these privacy devices anyway. Minister's children would never get to talk to their parents at all if both parents were completely at the beck and call of the public. Even before they can talk, they make demands—I mean how many times can you answer the door while you're nursing your baby before both of you get the colic? Or suppose you are bathing your infant. On one such occasion I called out to a woman to please come on in because I was bathing the baby, which she could see through the window. She called back that she would come in when I came to the door. She would still be standing there if I had done what I wanted to, but instead I bundled up my baby and went to the door. A few incidents like that made me acutely aware that my children had rights and it was up to me to protect those rights—and sometimes create them. So if you are scared to control the crowd for your own sake, think of the kids. Maybe they need an uninterrupted story or game. Few people realize that your relationships with your children are constantly broken into, a thing they may well come to resent later on.

Well now! That was a gloomy note, and entertaining is supposed to be fun. Maybe your need is exactly the opposite. Maybe you are scared to death to invite anybody in (so you never do!). You've been cooking for only a year, you've been to such beautiful homes and yours looks a little shabby by comparison, you don't have any nice dishes and barely any money to buy extras. So begin small, but begin . . .

Let's suppose that it is entirely your option to invite a group to meet in your home (which it probably will be if you communicated well), and you would like to serve something. What do you know how to make? Popcorn? Men love popcorn, and their wives probably don't make it often because it gets all over the place. Instant success. Serve popcorn and ice water—just make it a little more elegant with wet napkins or finger bowls which, of course, you bring out first, making everyone wonder what on earth you are serving. Warning: make a lot.

After you've accomplished some innovative (only because you don't know anything else) evenings, you will have established a reputation for being a hostess who knows how to make food fun. From that, it is a simple step to a casual dinner, strictly buffet style—

maybe a cook-your-own barbecue where you provide the implements to cook with but don't actually do the cooking. That gets you off the hook neatly. If the meat is burned, it's their fault! You, of course, can't afford the meat so you invite everybody to bring his own—and you provide the rest of the dinner. This isn't recommended for entertaining the Church Magnificents, but it works for a church school class or couples' club. The more informal, the less chance of doing something wrong —unless you have a waffle party and blow all the circuits in the house, or you make homemade ice cream and it doesn't freeze completely, or the drain plugs solid just before everybody arrives, or the oven refuses to light, or . . . relax! Those things happen to everybody, not just you! They don't even count!

From the patio to the dining room is one gigantic step—you may want to modify it by pausing for a few kitchen events. Do you know a couple well enough to ask them to join a family meal? That way you cook exactly the same things you always do, set the table as though nothing is happening, and entertain without alerting your inner warning system. Of all events, this one pays the most dividends. Everybody loves a kitchen table because he immediately feels at home (how can you help feeling at home with the baby knocking over her milk and the dog waiting patiently for any scrap of food that might fall from a fumbling hand?). Just be prepared to talk awhile. Kitchen dinners have a way of causing people to sit and talk for hours. Resist the temptation to move to the living room too soon, because unless the conversation is really going well, the shift to a more formal room may kill all the spontaneity. How can you get your point across if you haven't got a table to lean your elbows on?

At last you feel ready to take on a formal dinner— sort of. If you still shake at the prospect, go halfway. Use the dining room and your good china but serve family style. Later—when you are really organized— you can try the seven-course thing. Right now family-style service keeps you more at the table and relaxes your guests a little. And speaking of guests—better keep it small. (The budget will appreciate this also.) Two couples are a whole lot easier to entertain than five!

Cut even that number in half when you do the whole bit: crystal, china, sterling, linen, seven courses inter-spersed with much music, candlelight, and camaraderie. If you're the timid type, practice on one couple you know well—it will be a way of saying you want to do some-thing special for them, and meantime they are unwit-tingly doing a special thing for you. They are giving you confidence and experience, paving the way for the Grand Dinner Party. Never having gotten this far myself, I must assume that the pinnacle might be a sit-down din-ner for twenty with seven courses, immaculately designed place settings, prize-winning centerpieces, and food that matches the finest cuisine in the world. When you do it, drop me a line and let me know how it comes out.

Now that you have completed this handy course of entertaining with grace (that's what you say before meals because, otherwise, you might not have any!), let us take a quick review of much simpler but moderately effective ways of opening your home. These have various headings: brunches, bring-in salad luncheons, potluck dinners to name a few. The epitome of entertaining with minimal skill can be reached in this category. You don't have to cook much, if at all, and the crowd is the thing. People come for the company, and the food is incidental. These events take up the whole house because, to get everybody in, you need the space. Therefore, your culinary skills are not nearly so important as how well you clean your house—and control your children after you've cleaned it. I still see the face of a slightly amused woman who asked me if I had seen the bathroom lately. The alarm flag shot up and, upon investigation, there was good cause. My two-year-old had been busy decorating the bathroom walls, tub, mirror, sink, doors, and light switches with lipstick while I had been decorating the table!

Nevertheless, here is ease in entertaining. A small group of women meet in your home for a circle meeting and enjoy a yummy coffee cake served from a simple table. Buy it or bake it. They are so busy talking that almost any food becomes merely an added pleasure to the morning. And the famous potluck supper means coffee, tea, and bread—maybe. How simple can entertaining get—and for that matter, how cheap?

It is altogether possible, however, that none of this is for you. You work, or you can't be bothered, or you can't afford anything at all more than once a year. I admit to having entertained in all the above ways, but I also admit that a small dose of entertaining goes a long way for me. My ideal is one simple menu that everybody likes, used over and over, but never with the same people! Except for one thing. I work for days on it. Every crystal drop is polished, every wooden surface shines, the dog is banned, and the kids are groomed. Things move at a feverish pitch as the day arrives. Even the garage gets cleaned! There is just nothing like it to put everything shipshape. I fall into bed exhausted but immensely pleased the night before. Nothing has been missed, and for the only time in the year the whole house shines. Tomorrow is Open House!

The parsonage committee or the parsonage hostesses are usually on hand helping in the kitchen —often supplying the cookies and canapés. Refreshments are simple, but for the house it is no holes unbared! (Actually, we don't encourage closet and drawer opening, but it has been known to happen.) The guided tours include everything from the pictures hanging on the wall to the latest sewing project under production. The kids talk to everybody, show off their rooms, their models, aquariums, and what-have-you; and if it is a new house or if it has been redecorated, we have even been known to give everybody a price list of church expenditures. Last time the napkins read "Welcome to your house and our home!" If the church owns the house, here is your chance to prove you are a responsible tenant. It also opens up all kinds of interests hidden among the church people—they see something you do and begin to tell you what they do. They stay only as long as they want to, and nobody talks business. In one fell swoop you have accomplished giving everybody a chance to be entertained in your home, and the rest of the year you can go about your living in peace. Open House is a lot of work, a lot of fun, and a great conscience pacifier for nonentertainers like me.

There are two small areas we have neglected: your habits and your husband. Maybe you have a language barrier, making it utterly impossible for you to speak to your kids without turning the volume up full or sprinkling the sentences with tiny words of the four-letter variety. Either of these speak-easy habits is guaranteed to destroy the mood of the finest dinner—and maybe your husband's ministry. A serious study of chapter ten is recommended in dealing with this condition.

No matter how far into Women's Lib you are, sooner or later you'll have to come to grips with housekeeping. When you trip over the clutter en route to the door, have to clean off a spot for your visitor to sit, and can't find a clean coffee cup in the kitchen mess, you possibly have a problem! But not with housecleaning. Check what you think of yourself, the condition of your marriage, and your general mental attitude. Whom are you trying to hurt by the constant clutter? You? Your husband? The church? Living in these conditions is well nigh impossible and entertaining downright incredible.

Then, there's your husband. You may or may not be blessed with a man who comes home two hours early on the night ten couples are coming to dinner, and it may or may not be a blessing if he does come home. When it comes to entertaining, men, and in particular your man, can be most unpredictable. He's a minister, right? He works with people, right? He keeps a precise schedule, right? Wrong. You can almost bet your sterling that the night of the big event some couple will decide to break up their marriage. Now, if you haven't considered this beforehand, they might succeed in breaking up yours, too. You simply have to resist comparing your man to all the other men you have seen helping their wives in the kitchen, serving hor d'oeuvres to the guests, pouring coffee, and otherwise being the amiable host. The only safe thing to do when you are married to a man who may or may not even arrive for the party (though he usually will or else!) is to plan to do it all yourself and consider yourself blessed if he gets free to lend a hand. That way you don't end up feeling sorry for yourself or hating him—maybe a teeny bit angry, but not hating him.

At such times of stress it is tempting to get your dander up so that when he walks in the door you virtually accost him—but that's not the way. Stay cool and calm, carry off the evening in grand style, and when the guests have left, then accost him. After all, husbands should know they're needed, and how will they know if we don't tell them? Actually, by the time the evening is finished you will be too tired to be angry, and his completely outlandish reason for being late will provide an interesting postscript to the night. Rest assured that next time he'll be there if he can, but expect the scenario to repeat many times with slightly different twists. So either way, it's interesting. The secret is to plan it without him and let him be the serendipity of your affair. (Take that any way you want to!)

I always said that if a bishop ever came to the door everything would be a mess—and it was! To make it worse, the same man returned the following week and caught me in my robe with curlers in my hair. But in what other common life could you entertain the small and great of the world? Missionaries, bishops, space researchers, an African princess, people of all colors and nations have graced our home—with many more yet to come. For a girl who twenty-one years ago couldn't cook beans so they wouldn't bounce on the plate, that's progress—measurable and immeasurable. The cooking arts can be measured, but the gift of people to us and our children could never be measured in a lifetime.

Entertaining is an art. With a little practice you may succeed in producing a lifelong masterpiece. Just think —you and the Mona Lisa!

9
The Love of Money
Is Sin

"Let the preacher's wife have the first pick!"

The words still ring in my ears nineteen years later. The scene? The annual rummage sale of our student church. Spread before me were all the attic and basement treasures of our community: the sat-in dresses, the out-of-style hats, soul-sprung shoes, weathered purses, and enough bric-a-brac to keep me dusting for a generation. And I was to get first choice!

There was only one problem. I didn't want any of it. I didn't even like the idea of a rummage sale in the church—it was a desecration of the temple to my way of thinking. The whip tingled in my hand to drive the money changers out of the House of the Lord! Why couldn't they just give of their means—or even tithe? (Breathe that last word softly!) Why this farce of charity?

Lots of rummage sales have come and gone. A few bazaars have had their day (less of those because they take more dedicated work and planning, I think). I remain unconvinced that this is the way to pay the temple dues, but my pride has been shaken many a time so that infrequently I purchase an article or two. I finally had to admit that since I am not very rich, maybe even borderline poor, I had better be a very good shopper— and so had you . . .

Timothy gives us a way to be rich in the parsonage: "grow rich in noble actions" (I Timothy 6:18 NEB). The problem is that you can't eat your actions. Your words, maybe—but then you'll surely have indigestion. And there you are: sweet, innocent, trusting your husband to provide (first mistake), and confident that the paycheck will come at the end of every pay period (second mistake), and it will take care of all your needs (strike three; you're out!).

Your husband doesn't provide—the church does. Except in a few cases the people decide how much—or how little—your wages will be and when you will receive them. This process is quite dependable and usually as generous as the local congregation can afford to be, but you may not be able to afford as much as *they* can. The second part of the process may be a little more erratic since it depends on a volunteer treasurer and sometimes on his particular habits of punctuality or life circumstances or what he thinks of your husband's ministry. Fortunately, his kind are dying out, but deserve a mention before they become extinct altogether. Some treasurers view the money of the church as their personal property, so you must negotiate for your paycheck. Maybe it is the only way they ever get a pastoral call, and it insures at least one a month. Meanwhile, you wait patiently for your check to arrive by mail or at the door and finally make a frantic call to find out that the check has been there all the while, but the procedure in this church is for your husband to pick it up. Now, don't get ticked! Most of the employees in the world have to go to the paymaster to get their checks. The only difference is that his pay window is in his house. Your mistake was in not finding out how you were to be paid. It is a business matter, not personal, and that's the way it ought to be handled—from the head.

Sometimes, no matter how the church people wish it otherwise, there just isn't enough money in the coffers to pay you. Before you lay blame on your husband for not doing his work or your parishioners for being stingy, get a firm grip on the whole scene. Your income is based on volunteer giving. If the flu has been through your community, doctor bills go up and contributions go down. Unemployment signals an immediate drop-off in income. So, unfortunately, do sermons that are poorly prepared or highly controversial. Maybe it's the end of the year and apportionments or mission-giving or taxes are coming due, or a million other church expenses have drained the pot. Since inflation is a continuing force in society, the church and you must cope with this as well. So your paycheck may be less or late.

More likely to affect you is the actual amount of wages received. You can receive them promptly, hand-delivered to your doorstep, but if they are insufficient to your needs, you're still in trouble. You have just three alternatives: your expenditures have got to be cut, your shopping skills sharpened, or your income increased. (A fourth alternative is to leave the ministry, and if the love of money is the only reason, see chapter ten.)

Cutting expenses takes very objective assessment. In the first place, you have to decide what is need and what is luxury, especially since most luxuries appear as necessities in advertising. (You *need* a color TV since your eyes are not equipped to register color without the aid of the set, right?) Objectivity has no room for rationalizing your wants or justifying your purchases on the grounds that your husband bought his skis, so why can't you buy a new dress? Power plays are definitely OUT and cooperation is definitely IN.

You need food, but do you need steak? You need clothes, but must they be name labels or even brand new, for that matter? You need electricity, but does the house have to be lit up at night so that passing planes won't crash into it? That's not even good ecology! Got the picture? The two of you sit down and have a loving discussion about what you can change in your life-style, either actual or still desired, so that the paycheck fits. After you have kissed and made up, you may be able to establish a budget . . .

One economist's approach to budget is to keep track of everything you spend for three months, and then determine what amounts you require for everything. Provided you haven't gone broke or accumulated the national debt in those three months, it might work. A simpler way is to go to your local bank, many of which have financial counselors or free budget books that will objectively put you on the path to good cents. If you feel intimidated because the bank president is chairman of the church board, then go to the next town or to the library and check out a book on managing household finances. The guidelines are written down so that all you have to do is manipulate them to fit your life-style. This is a good idea even if your income is totally adequate. Lots of marriages stand or fall over what happens to the paycheck, so why not check your pay before it comes to that?

Armed with a budget, or at least a system of handling your meager hoard, and having examined your needs and wants, you may have discovered that the major flaw is neither your good intentions nor your planning. It may be your psyche . . .

Getting psyched out over money is easy enough to do (just drop me a million any day and see me go wild!), but recognizing it as your problem is more difficult. For example, you feel penned in by little children, you don't have your family nearby, you haven't made any close friends yet, so you treat yourself to a night out. Good therapy—but not four times a month! Or you don't carry cash so you won't spend it, but decide to get an item you have wanted secretly—only this time you use your credit card. After all your debt limit is $1,500 on that card, and you only owe $250; at $10 a month, the payments are really easy. Or a salesman knocks at your door. He is delightful to talk to, and plainly his product is an excellent one. This really isn't the time you had planned to buy such a thing, but someday you did want it, so why not now? You'll manage it somehow. Besides your husband isn't there to help you say no, and the salesman needs just one more sale to make his $1,000 bonus, and you would be doing a Christian act for him. (Never mind that you might cause your husband to sin by losing his religion in anger!)

Impulse spending is the downfall of the poor. In fact, it keeps them poor. The poorer you are the better target you make because there is so much more to want. Add easy credit and long-term payments to this, plus a little financial ignorance, and you are in debt forever. So look yourself right in the face (a mirror will help with that one!) and say, "Look here. We are going to live within our income, and don't you forget it." Then repeat it to your husband . . . and your teen-agers . . . and the dog . . . and go right out to buy yourself an account book. Get a big one that will last a lifetime, and it will become a family history as well.

Make your first-page entry a historic one. Tell who you are, something about your family background, your children, your ministry. Begin as if there were no ending—because there never will be. Keeping books is the most unending process I know, and just possibly you aren't the one suited to do it. In that loving discussion you had, you should have decided who is best at bookkeeping and has the time to do it. If you share the task, set up a regular schedule shaped to the church year— you do Christmas and Easter and he can do June and July while you chase the kids.

Why keep books? An obvious necessity if you ever get dragged into court for income-tax evasion or libel or bankruptcy, but beyond those highly facetious possibilities bookkeeping can be your best ally. A limited income requires more control than an adequate one, especially if you take the injunction to be a good steward of the Lord. That is, biblically put, if your family is a tithing family. (You haven't considered tithing yet? Better study chapter ten!) Tithing is an assumption of the inner man, and there is no better time to begin tithing than as you begin your ministry or marriage. You will have to decide for yourself whether you include only taxable income or the whole paycheck as it arrives, plus that bigger decision of what you will use the tithe for. Hopefully, the latter will vary from time to time so that tithing becomes a joyful experience. It is really great to have the Lord's money available when someone is in need. I confess to having used some tithe money occasionally on the parsonages we lived in simply because no one else could see the need. The fruits of that tithe money are still being enjoyed by families who have followed us in various houses. Then sometimes I simply purchased items for the parsonage out of our own means, sent a check through the treasurer and a bill at the same time, so that for income tax purposes the giving was recorded but for my inner purposes my giving was beyond my tithe. But what has this to do with bookkeeping?

When the money arrives at our house, the full amount is set down at the beginning of that month's page of accounting. The next figure is tithe, written out and recorded in a special section at the back of the book for tithing expenditures only. Then comes "Household Expenses." It, too, is recorded at the back of the account book. This figure is derived by adding together all the regular large payments that come due around the year and then dividing them by twelve—months, that is. It includes life and health insurance, income tax and social security, auto insurance and license fees, church pension and death benefit payments, and an amount set aside for Christmas spending. The amount now remaining in my account book is the figure entered as deposit in my working checkbook. This is the money actually available for everyday expenditures without putting either the Lord's money or the "big bills" money in jeopardy. When checks are written for either of these two categories, they are recorded in the check book but marked with a "T" or "H" in the balance spot and subtracted only from their own accounts in the Big Book. An extra advantage to this system is that, when an emergency does arise, you have a balance in the bank to draw on without borrowing money (like almost every month), or overwriting your account. However, a cardinal rule is to put back any "overwrite" *first*, before anything else is paid, on the very next pay day.

My way may not be your way—or anybody else's—but it's a system that works. You and your beloved must find what works for you—and that goes for more than budgeting. Wow, are there a lot of things to be settled! Take credit cards, for instance—who gets which one, and how much do you get to use it? How many should you have in the first place (after awhile you can't close your wallet for the bulge)? Are you of the variety that can't resist seeing the clerk roll the little machine across your card? Maybe you ought to throw them all away! Credit cards often yield chronic bills that then can be solved by a consolidation loan that makes your payment so small each month that you decide to invest in a major purchase like the new car you've been waiting for. Then your daughter has the audacity to get seriously ill, and medical bills begin to mount. You think about consolidating your loans again, only to discover that the payment now would just about finish off your paycheck. If you think those sentences were long, the payments will be longer.

Debt is like a cancer. It grows swiftly, consumes your happiness, can kill your marriage, and makes you suffer a lot. Sometimes the only alternative is to learn to be poor and happy at the same time, or for you to go to work. Thank goodness, the day of the Super Frown has passed! That's the one the church people or the Ecclesiastical Brass gave you when you announced you were working. Everyone *knew* that a minister and his wife were hired as a team to serve the church, and somehow, by bringing income from a source other than the church, you no longer belonged to the team. The faulty reasoning was theirs—when you brought in the extra income, you often lifted the load off your over-burdened husband and took the pressure off the church to raise your salary. You were also able to increase your giving. Unfortunately, such pragmatic reasoning was rarely acceptable, and the wife returned to the kitchen that suddenly had become a prison. Now, we live in the Enlightened Latter Days. The wives of our laymen have gone to work also, so what can they say? Like any woman who works, you must examine whether you will gain real income after such expenses as child care and clothes, etc. If you have no marketable skills, your time might be more profitably spent going to school to ac-quire these so that your income level will be higher when you do go to work—but that's another chapter. Suffice it to say that work is one alternative to the budget crisis.

If you have three under three, it isn't a very viable alternative anyway. And maybe you *like* staying at home. Fine! Learn to receive and learn to do or at least make do. Somewhere in your church or community is someone who will teach you to sew (in case you missed home economics on the way up). You might even or-ganize a class in your church or home so that the local school system will provide a teacher. Make it a mission teach-and-sew class. As you learn, you make garments to send to the mission field. That way your material comes out of tithe money, you are more careful to do it right, and you feel doubly good about the finished product. Innovate a pattern swap within the women's society. Take a course in fabrics and tailoring through the local night school program. Don't be too proud to go through garments someone has given you and recut or resize them for further wear. You might even find this variety at the rummage sale (God forbid!).

Shop the want ads and garage sales. Make discount houses and outlets your favorite haunts—but not until you have become well acquainted with quality products sold in large department stores. You must be able to recognize the quality potential in every purchase, or you will find yourself with a closet full of sleazy clothes that get hip-sprung in the first wearing or lose their shape with the first washing. You are then considerably worse off for wear . . .

Apply the same innovative techniques to furniture, bikes, anything you must buy. Look before you leap. Don't hesitate to borrow other people's knowledge about certain items—remember it is a blessing for them to give. (*Forced* giving bestows very little blessing, however. Be wise.)

Through it all, look good! Some of us naturally look better than others, but even the best can generally use help. Throw a makeup party or go in for a free demonstration. Watch how the makeup is applied, resist the sales pitch (or buy *one* item if your conscience hurts), and go down to your local drug or dime store to see what you can match from the sale bin. Models do it; why not you?

Then, there is that constant stress—hair! It must be cut, curled, blown dry, colored, or set just so. This applies to not only your hair, but to your husband's also. The price of men's haircuts is phenomenal, even if they wear it longer nowadays. In fact, it costs more because it must be styled, just like yours. Hair can be a major item in the budget if you're not careful. You might try learning to cut your husband's hair. Start with the boys if you have any; otherwise, wait till a *long* vacation. For yourself, find a good beauty school close by. Their prices are half those of professional shops, and senior students sometimes do better work because a supervisor is breathing down their necks. If that isn't available, see if you can trade hair care, with someone in the church who is skilled, for babysitting or something else she needs done. Or try a put-on! Hair pieces are often a good investment. They can be bought on sale, and if they are styled once every three months or so you can always look nice. This budget item can be a hair-raising situation (sorry!).

Quality is the key. Especially for your husband's clothes! Men's suits are major items in any budget, but quality must not be compromised here. You can buy a dress of lower quality because you wear it less. Not so your husband (he'd look silly in a dress anyway). His suits must be on the go every day in all kinds of weather—sat in, stood in, knelt in, eaten in. They need to be wrinkle-proof, stain-resistant, long-wearing, and non-fading. (Double knees for heavy pray-ers are hard to find.) Slacks can also be washable to cut the cleaning bill. All these clothes can still be bought at sale prices or through discount houses or buyers' clubs. Be alert to sales, and save the money so you are prepared to purchase. (Resist the temptation of jealousy when you pay $89.95 for his suit and your most expensive dress cost $9.00 at the outlet store. He has to wear his *every* day.)

By now you have your clothes right, your hair is stylish, your makeup perfect, but look at the old heap you're driving around in! Try washing it first. And a good wax job might improve the scene. Cars are the temptation of a man's life. My husband is always having affairs with his. They get so attached to him that when *I* try to drive them they won't even start! One particular sweetheart decided to run her windshield wipers all the way downtown and back with no regard to my frantic efforts to stop them. And it wasn't even raining. For him, of course, they were completely normal. I used to console myself that at least *those* affairs didn't reproduce, but now I'm not so sure. The driveway gets more crowded all the time . . .

Affairs or no, a car, and sometimes two, is a necessity. And, oh, the expense! Convince your husband he ought to take a course in auto mechanics—it will save hundreds of dollars (provided your marriage stays intact!). If he resists, remind him of the sewing skills you have acquired with much loss of patience and aching shoulders. Should that not prevail, look for a good, inexpensive auto mechanic (there may not be any in America, but somewhere . . .).

Buying an automobile new is a great temptation, but it costs a thousand dollars' depreciation to go around the block. The Lord's Prayer is handy here, especially the line about "lead me not into temptation." There was a beautiful yellow Plymouth convertible sitting on the showroom floor of a place I passed every day on my way to work. We were about to graduate from seminary and move to a warmer climate, and I was sure that car should go with us. It did, but not before a major blizzard almost buried it and we became the brunt of much laughter among our classmates. Shortly afterward we moved across the country, and I jackknifed the trailer we were pulling into the tailfin of our yellow beauty (my only accident in twenty years!). Then we were assigned to the mountains where rain and snow were our constant winter companions. Three years and many ruts later we sold it for a piece of junk. The youth fellowship had clambered over its sides, the hills had claimed its motor, and the weather had faded its glow. We finished paying for it about the time we bid farewell. *Then* we were sent to the valley, where the weather reached a hundred degrees . . . Since then, my husband has picked out the cars.

Does this story have a moral? In a book like this? Of course. Let someone else depreciate, not you! You can smugly drive a late model car, knowing that you are a thrifty and careful shopper . . . with a few tips from your friendly local mechanic on the condition of the purr under the hood. If none of them are friendly, invest a few dollars in his time to take him along on the final selection trip. Saves millions (evangelistically speaking, that is). The head lady at the local library will be stunned to find you poring over old consumer magazines as if your life depended on it—and it may, especially if you buy a car that had a major brake fault that year! Remember, you are looking for a real break!

Then there's the curse of the everyday budget—the Gas Hog. If you are lucky enough to own one of these, you may hallucinate visions of your car eagerly chasing from station to station just so it can snuggle up to one of those cute little pumps with the long extension cords that give such a large charge. The only trouble is that for you the charge may be more than you can stand. As gasoline becomes more scarce, the present prices will soon be "the good old days," so ask, "Does this car go more than ten miles on a gallon of gas?" If the answer is "thirty," your hubby may just have found his calling— car, that is.

If you happen to be a heavy-load-pulling family, you may have to scratch that gassy luxury and settle for fewer miles and more go power. Some of our friends seem to go away fairly frequently with trailers tagging behind. All that ever manages to trail behind us is the hopeful hitch, for vacations are few and far between. If you are the once-a-year variety, you might look into renting a vacation vehicle in order to save money all year (to rent the vacation vehicle, maybe . . .).

A final consideration, at least in this book, is the question of hauling the church kids. It is very easy to become the local Sunday School Bus or the prior-agreement vehicle to hire free to go to the beach. This is a tremendous advantage for the church—specifically for the parents of youth involved who prefer to stay home and watch TV football. It solves all kinds of family problems caused by nagging father to "go help the young people," or attempting to eliminate the generation gap caused by young people wanting to do something live and physical when their parents groan just getting out of the chair to go to the refrige. You will not, of course, become endangered with such groaning since, if your auto is of sufficient size, you will go skiing, beaching, camping, backpacking, canoeing, work camping . . . You will make a lovely specimen in your casket! But no matter, you will die happy since anybody knows that a minister and his wife *love* to do these things, else why did they go into the work? Possibly you were ignorant of such bliss and find that you really prefer to stay home with your own children, or you may be cursed with the feeling that these young people have parents who ought to be responsible for working with the group. The only cure for such thoughts is to buy a small car, big enough for your family and that's all. Lot's of ministers do. I've seem them on my way back from the beach . . .

Trust in the Lord—and the church agencies—when medical crisis arrives. Maybe the state will help because you end up eligible for welfare. Somehow with our household slush fund and the few pennies we save, we have managed to squeak through the Med Feds—not, however, without a real sense of knowing that God will provide. The church can help with a good health insurance policy; if it isn't good, kick up some fuss until it gets one. But it won't cover everything, and you shouldn't expect it to. Teeth have to be fixed, ears examined, coughs diluted—all at trickles of money that sometimes threaten to flood your budget altogether. If you're the scared type, throw a little extra into the household account for medical bills; socialized medicine will take its own sweet time. Our family of six has managed to spend $380 per year over a ten-year period. Before you panic, that's just $55 a person for dentists, doctors, and drugs, plus the fact that three have had major surgery and another was hit by a car. Indeed, this is a very low figure! Good health is the ultimate of blessings, but when the blessing is withdrawn, you have to pay the bills—so be ready!

Then, there is education. Such a field day it has with your meager resources! Avoid foolish promises, no matter how heartfelt . . . like telling your children you will *give* them their college education. You may end up like me, working my head off to pay college bills—for thirteen years I'll be working if they all go, and for four of those years there will be two in at once! Lucky for me, I like to work! You may or may not be able to. Even if college isn't their thing, trade schools are expensive as well. Plan now to pay later! Your credit card doesn't cover *everything*. Maybe you have a work skill that is getting rusty because you're not using it—better keep it polished. Insurance helps if you can afford it when you're struggling on minimum salary. Also, you have twelve good years to say, "Study, study, study," which makes for lousy family relationships but nets scholarships. The last method is very risky since it depends on good genes, and your family tree may not always produce Grade A fruit.

Of course, when they are little children, you can always qualify for Headstart. This is a great assist in getting the salary raised as well. One church we served had Headstart and private nursery school going in adjacent rooms. If it hadn't been for the discount the church gave us, our child would have been in Headstart, which was why the discount. It was a delicious occasion when salary deficiency was very obvious in a fairly affluent community! But don't be proud. If you qualify for state aid and your family needs it, just figure that you add to the taxpayers' blessings by causing them to contribute to the church when they really never meant to. On second thought, there may be better ways of raising the salary . . . but if not, don't hesitate!

The obvious expenditure of every household is food —so obvious that it merits little discussion since you can read anywhere how to scrape by—by scraping plates. Welcome any blessing from heaven that falls after the women's society luncheon—it may keep you from starving. Take your *whole* family to the potlucks and instruct them to eat a LOT—discreetly, of course. Go to everything where food will be served, and tell the person who is going to such a meeting to eat less at the table that night. Have your husband schedule breakfast meetings where the food is provided by the women's circles. You don't have to feed him that way. Work at all the dinners so you can take home leftover food. If milk is a major item, buy a cow—she will keep your lawn mowed, your family supplied with milk products, and your roses fertilized. (That last by-product might become a nifty little money-raising item but is definitely not the homemade donation for the bazaar . . .)

If you've done all of the above and the budget still doesn't stretch far enough, then try doing the more regular things like buying a used freezer so you can get day-old bread (like new when thawed), buy in larger quantities, and go shopping less often. The fewer times you go through the grocery store door, the better off you are. Milk is always at the back of the store, so you have to pass the goodies in between. Budget-smashers planned it that way! Outfox them. Get your milk at the dairy so you don't see those temptations. And plan, plan, plan. If you know exactly what you need, you have a better chance of planning great meals for less money. When all is said and done, if beans are the best you can do, make an event out of them—put on your best china, crystal, silver, and candlelight. Nobody will be able to see what he is eating but will be firmly convinced it must be a delicacy for you to have gone to such trouble.

Above all, don't give up hope. In a century or two minister's salaries will be higher. You will be dead by then, but everybody has to pioneer a cause! Meantime, learn to live with what you've got and enjoy having it.

If you live in America, you have more wealth than 90 per cent of the world's people anyway, and you're the rich one. The love of money is sin—so be thankful you can be saved from such a dereliction. Meantime, use every nickel, dime, and penny you can lay your hands on!

10
Meditate! Meditate! Meditate!

Maintaining your spiritual life in the parsonage is most difficult. Now mind, I didn't say religious life! That is the easiest thing of all. If you participate in the church in the least, you can have an exemplary religious life, what with teaching in the church school, or sinning (whoops! singing) in the choir, or simply being there every Sunday—Bingo! Grade AA, Extra Large Religious Life.

But having a spiritual life is a whole other collection plate.

It is very easy to be religious and hate the church members.

It is very easy to be religious and resent the parsonage committee.

It is very easy to be super-religious (translate "extra active in church work") and hate yourself—or your husband, who got you into this mess.

Of course, if you choose to do the religious thing, you'll die young of shriveled spirit—or any of a host of other diseases that spring from bitterness and hatred. This will evoke many kind phrases at your funeral like, "Isn't it strange? She was such a *good* woman, so active in her church, and so loyal to her husband. A pity she had to die so young!" If that compliment isn't to your liking, you can console yourself that a whole church full of women will soon be actively engaged in seeking a new wife for your husband and mother for your "poor orphaned darlings." Of course, this will complicate your husband's ministry for a while, what with all those women out to trap him, but you can chuckle in your grave about the problems he is having to hassle with and the trials his new wife will so unexpectedly enter. All grave thoughts, of course, in the best religious tradition . . .

Fortunately, you don't have to be the offering of sacrifice! Let's face it; you don't qualify anyway since you are not single and no longer a virgin, both of which are requirements for human religious sacrifice in pagan beliefs. (The pagan part might fit, since, without a spiritual life, you are.) But finding your way out of sacrifice and into service may be a long, hard struggle, for it has the prerequisite of facing the fact that you stand in need of the redeeming grace of Jesus Christ, and that humbling acknowledgment can get all messed up with your husband's preaching and theology—and your marriage relationship. If you start out Sunday morning by being confronted with the fact that there is no white shirt in the closet, and "Oh, yes, I forgot to tell you; I invited So-and-so to dinner," when it's the end of the month and he *knows* you're out of food; and three children to get ready alone because their *father* has already left; and you have to be there early for a quick teachers' meeting and the baby spills oatmeal all down the front of your only good dress, any inspiration from your husband's sermon has long since been wiped out for you by the time you finally sink into your seat. You may even sit there and muse about the absurdity of it all—that you are supposed to cook for, clean for, pick up after, wash dirty socks of, raise children of, and engage in sex with the very same man whom you must now magically transform into your spiritual adviser. This is especially difficult if you know that, after the service is over and everyone is at home, he is bound to wait anxiously for your opinion of his message.

Now, any of the above could hinder spiritual growth, not to mention marital bliss, and the great temptation is to tell yourself you are quite a woman to be able to carry all this load for the cause of Christ. That is your second mistake—pride. But the first one was to let yourself get in this situation in the first place. You need to take yourself in hand.

A spiritual search is a personal one, and so you must begin by knowing the person you actually are (back to chapter one)—not the preacher's wife, which may be the role you play. Lots of wives get the feeling that if someone took a picture of them the way they see themselves, they would faintly resemble a body splattered against a concrete wall, arms and legs stretched to their extremes, with the spirit leaking out of all the cracks and holes. And when they say they need to pull their Self together, they are judging the condition accurately.

Please notice, the word I used was "wives," not "ministers' wives," because it happens to any woman who doesn't periodically take the time to examine what she is doing, and why, and whether or not her life patterns are nourishing her spirit or draining it. Such an act requires contemplation and courage because it may mean that you will have to start limiting yourself to specific areas, saying "no" to church members (who probably are asking you to do things because you always say "yes" and it saves them the trouble of coaxing someone else to do the job), and resolving that Puritan-ethic guilt which says you can't possibly be a Christian unless you answer every need and work all the time. Try this one on: it is totally selfish of you to attempt to cover all the bases in the church because you then prevent someone else (who may have to be coaxed) from developing his leadership potential or find his personal worth. And selfishness is SIN.

It is also selfish of you to tie up your time so that you can't play with your children . . . or the dog . . . or walk on the beach occasionally . . . or follow your own career training . . . or crochet . . . or sit down in the middle of a messy house and make a banner that says "Joy!" . . . or whatever your thing is. You are being selfish to your own inner being, denying it the surging joy of life that Christ came to give.

Now, of course, you may not be that woman wound up in activity. You may be caught in the second mistake of pride for just the opposite reason. You take great pride in being an entirely separate woman, doing her own thing and leaving her husband to carry his job alone just as any other man does. Well, that would be cool if your husband had a job like any other man's. The trouble is, he doesn't.

No matter how you cut it, unless your husband is a celibate, which obviously he isn't, he needs you. (*How* he needs you is something else again. Maybe you gossip, and he needs you to go off and do your own thing as far away from the church as possible!) So part of finding your spiritual self is to know him from the standpoint of his needs and expectations. How does he *really* want you to fit into his life and work? Maybe you will discover that he resents your doing all the frantic activity bit even more than you do! What a shocker that would be! Or perhaps he needs you to give just a little and come further into his life so that his burdens are easier to cope with. Marriage based on honest, loving communication has a chance to grow into a life experience of great beauty—especially in the parsonage where you must so constantly give yourself away to others that your partner can become your source of tender loving care and spiritual renewal.

So begin your search by finding out who you are and who you want to be, and who your husband is and who he wants you to be. By now, you may be angry that anyone would even suggest that your husband has a right to say what he wants you to be, what with women's lib and self-actualization the thing today. In that case, your anger may tell you something about the state of your marriage or even your spiritual life. At any rate, whatever your position on women's lib, you are in fact married to the guy, so why not consider what he has to say? It may even open the door between the two of you which will lead to a whole new life-style.

Just as your personal life has to develop, so does your spiritual commitment have to deepen. For it not to do so spells disaster for your marriage and your life. You'll make it for awhile, depending on how Christian your husband is, and how determined you are to keep your marrige intact, but why struggle when you can do it the enrichment way? Christ promised an abundant life. You've made a step toward this abundance if you've enriched your personal life, but there is a catch: abundant life is promised to those who follow him, and it's for real!

So pray the Prayer of Surrender. Here I am, Lord. Use me anyway you want to, even in this awful town I'm stuck in. Open me up and use me for your glory.

And then make it a daily habit. Every morning, begin by giving your life over to God: "Use me today." Strange, wonderful things will happen. Suddenly you have new opportunities to be a Christian. You've surrendered to God, so you know he helps you have the courage and strength to do new things, to express yourself. If you get criticized, check out your methods of operation and if they are good, let God have the criticisms and keep right on going. There are more important things in God's world to be concerned about than criticism.

If you are serious about being surrendered, you have a new role. You're not a preacher's wife any more! Instead, you are Mary Smith, Christian person, whose husband happens to make his vocation the ministry. If it helps, introduce yourself without a tag like "my husband is the minister of the community church." If you do that, you're asking for a special place, and it's the very place that tied you in knots. Risk just being "you" in new groups. I'm Mary Smith, period. Feel insecure? Good! Now *you* have to perform; *you* have to emerge. Oh, I know that eventually someone will rat on you and word will get around that "she's the minister's wife," but by that time they will know *you* so it won't make any difference. And a gentle hint to a few people that you would like to be introduced by just your name, without the tag "minister's wife," is often helpful.

On the other hand, don't resent it when people do

144

introduce you as "our minister's wife." Let them, and wallow in the compliment intended, for they mean to express pride in you and your achievements. And achieve you will if you've taken these steps. Every day will become a new adventure, holding new excitement. Praying "Here am I, Lord; use me" automatically cues the question, "I wonder what will happen today?" and life becomes fresh every day. Of course, there's a catch. The surrender prayer is only a beginning place, and if you really want to develop power in your life, your praying has to include a few more items.

Item One: Rejoice!—in the earth, in your children, in your abilities, in your husband, in your church and its people, in the sky or mountains or a lake or cornfield, or the cycles of the universe, or whatever moves you! But make the rejoicing habit Item One every day.

Item Two: Open yourself to receive energy. The energy of God, which also is called the Holy Spirit, really is meant to dwell in *you*. Practice opening yourself to this energy through praying for the strength of God to dwell in you and empower you for the day.

Beyond surrender, rejoicing, and energizing, *you* know your particular need. Maybe you are being criticized, and you need to pray for understanding—for you to understand the critic and the critic to understand you. Or perhaps your hang-up is that you just can't accept the person you are. We've talked about developing the abilities of your person, but sometimes our lack of self-acceptance is so deep that we have to begin by accepting God's acceptance of us—with all our faults and foibles. Besides, polishing all that's good and able and making the most out of what you have is really where it's at with God!

145

Now—are you ready for a giant step? "Go into your closet and shut the door." If you're a literalist in this day of sliding-door closets that are never big enough anyway, you're in trouble; but if you live in a busy parsonage with forty or fifty people a week demanding your time by phone and doorbell, you've *got* to find a closet! And meditate, meditate, meditate! Shut down your brain. Absolutely refuse to worry. Clear your head. Pray, "Here am I, Lord. Speak." Then listen. This takes practice, but fifteen minutes somewhere in every day will pay dividends.

At first your brain may just idle, but after awhile you'll be listening and actually hear. Not a voice from without, but one from within. *What* you hear will depend on who you are. Maybe an order to do something, perhaps a poem or song will burst in, or maybe a clear direction about a decision. But a learned listener will soon become a hearer of the Word. Also remember to be a grateful listener. Thank God for directions given; rejoice a little every time you pray. It keeps the energy flowing—in from God and out to others.

That's not all! It is not sufficient to empty the mind and leave it there after quiet listening. You have to refill it so it has a direction, and here's where the fun begins. Go to your closest bookseller or library and pick out four nonfiction titles you think sound challenging. Put all four wherever you most likely drop during the day—or if you never sit, put them by your bed. Then, take five to ten minutes every three or four hours to read from one of them. Try to keep at least two different authors' ideas going at once so that, as you work, the two will hold discussions in your mind and you will begin to grow again intellectually—independently of your husband's brain. Make a pact with yourself, however, to read completely two out of the four books. Then get four more.

If the library is far away, don't overlook the corner paperback supply or, for that matter, your husband's library. You may be surprised to discover that some of his books are actually interesting.

Now you are probably thinking, How does that make me more spiritual? The answer is simple: it doesn't because that is part one of a two-part reading program. It is the mind stretcher, the thought reorganizer, the new-vista opener to get you ready for the real heady stuff.

Part two should also consist of two or three books, all versions of the same. Try *Reach Out*, or *Good News For Modern Man*, or *The Living Bible*, or even *The Revised Standard Version*. The Bible appears under many titles nowadays, so if what you have tried to read seems dull, for goodness' sake, don't fight it! Switch . . . to a new way of saying old ideas—plus a free concept of how and when to read it.

A chapter a day doesn't necessarily keep the Devil away! It may take just one verse or one parable, held close in your mind all day, turned and basted with the ideas flowing in from your other reading until, when the day is done, you have a finished thought-product that exceeds your expectations.

There is a special dividend in using two-part mind-filling. If you're worried, your children are cross, or your husband is tense, you can take a peace break several times a day by deliberately choosing to think of the day's reading. It helps give perspective to the dailiness of life by providing you with an eternal point of view.

If you've gotten this far in your spiritual trek, you will discover that something is happening to you. Perhaps for the first time in your life you will actually *want* to talk to someone else about your faith. You may find that your understanding has made your husband's sermons better, or your mutual reading and conversations have. You could be surprised to hear yourself talking ideas with your teen-ager; or, best of all, someone might comment on how radiant and alive you are! After all, if you walk daily in the light of God, you are bound to radiate a *little* of it!

Inside, a more settled serene person will begin to emerge. Oh, your ideas and actions may change constantly, but you cannot meditate daily without touching base with the kingdom of heaven inside you. And that brings peace—the kind of peace Christ promised to leave with us. How long it takes depends on how real your prayer of surrender is and how regularly you follow up with reading, meditation, and prayer.

Same old story you've heard for years, right? You have to commit yourself, and then read the Bible and pray! Well, don't blame me; *I* didn't give the instructions. The only new part is the one we've ignored so long but is so pointed in the way Christ lived:

Go into the olive garden . . . pull the leaves around you . . . and

meditate!
meditate!
meditate!

11
The Original Eve

So you want to be free of it all? Eve had the same problem. Lazing around in all that idyllic beauty drove her absolutely wild with boredom, so when the handsome snake slithered upon the scene, she was ready for her awakening! Her mistake was in sharing the lusty apple with Adam. She could have kept him bewildered for centuries . . .

But instead she ensnared us all in the baby brigade, doomed us to lives of servitude before a superior (?) male (just because he was made first!), and set us to finding our homes outside the Garden of Eden. Woman has never been satisfied since. Millions of years later the bras are burning, the flags are waving, and pins and bumper stickers burgeoning to announce the dissatisfaction of woman. Eve was dreadfully deprived, having only an apple for protest. (If she could have used a bumper sticker, it would surely have read, "This car is a virgin. Keep your distance.") No such luck for us. The libbers are upon us, and we must come to terms with them—and ourselves.

The parsonage is rarely a penthouse, but you can surely get pent up in it. How many hundreds of meetings do you go to before you begin to feel a sense of futility about it all? So much energy expended month after month on the same people—planning programs, getting special music, making luncheons . . . Sooner or later you have to ask yourself, Is this what my life should be about? And, in spite of the constant flurry of activity and occasional spurts of excitement, you may make the amazing discovery that you feel empty, drained of the real you. Maybe you even begin to feel too protected, too cloistered, too separated from the rest of the world —and small wonder! Between your religion and your budget you may only rarely bump into life at its grittiest where people suffer without medical care, struggle to survive on totally inadequate incomes (you have a whole church to help *you*, remember), are hated because of the color of their skin or the lack of color, or go for months without a human hand reaching out to them. Someplace along the line you may discover that the mission field you have been talking about for years is only four blocks away and you're not really doing anything about it. Easy! Such a discovery can change your life . . .

Of course, your port of arrival in women's lib could be quite different. Let's suppose that you are an avid reader and everything you pick up says "Are You Truly Free?" or "How to Be Liberated and Not Get a Divorce," or "Is Your Marriage an Open Marriage?" Not too many titles have to confront you before you begin to wonder about your marital and personal condition of freedom, especially when the kids are crying, your husband has gone to *another* meeting, the phone is ringing, and your head is splitting. You catch a glimpse of a headline on the daily paper that reads "Youth Takes Back Door to Freedom" and you eye your own back door surreptitiously . . .

There is also the possibility that you have survived

The Last Wedding and find that your life has suddenly dropped in activity level. You were tired of cleaning house years ago—like how many times can you sweep the floor?—and your husband is rarely home, so what are you to do? Join the club for Senior Citizens at forty-five? Macrame eight hours a day? (Write?)

One small factor keeps you from finding an easy solution to your confrontation with meaning in your life —you have probably sat through more sermons and speeches about the needs of the world than any other lay person. You may even have been attracted to your husband because of his sense of urgency and mission which you have come to share. And then there is the biggest bugaboo of them all: to be a Christian you must be selfless, thinking of others; so how do you even think of your needs and wants without feeling guilty? Honey, you have got a problem!

My Bible reads, "I am come that they might have life, and that they might have it more abundantly." I just *have* to assume that the statement includes ministers' wives as well as other humans and that the rights and privileges of being a full person are mine for the claiming. I realize this may be full-scale heresy in some departments of the church, but stake-burning is not too prevalent today so I'm willing to take my chances. Confronted with emptiness within, one has to move out to abundance. It is time to walk out of the parsonage— by the *front* door.

Wait, though! While you're putting on your coat, consider a question: How much are you willing to give up in order to gain personal freedom? Your leisure time? Your easy lazy days? Your church involvement? Your companionship with your husband? . . . Your husband? !

If you go through that door to get away from an unhappy marriage, better face the fact now. Either you deal with the marriage and its needs with professional help or you eventually deal yourself out of the marriage. If that's what you're after, you might as well make it easier on everybody and exit the marriage instead of pretending to seek your new liberated self. You will end up with an old self that has a new set of excuses for putting distance between you and your husband. There *is* the potential, however, for becoming a happier person, which will cause your husband to fall in love with you all over again, giving the two of you a better marriage. Now, if that's your motivation, the result can be very positive so go ahead and button your coat.

Don't turn the door knob, though, until you decide if you are running away from the church and if so, why? Is the church the shyster who has stolen away your personal freedom, or are you afflicted with a crumbly backbone that could never stand up to people pressures? Take heed! If people have been walking over you for years, it will be rougher on the other side of that door where nobody cares about loving-kindness. The reason for running away is inside your coat, not in the church. Time to face SELF—revamp it completely if necessary. Time to come out from under that role of being the minister's wife and start being a person (you've heard it before, I know! I just can't stop saying it till you *do* it!).

Take a minute to look in the mirror hanging by the door. What kind of a face do you see? Full of hate, bitterness, resentment? Are you running out to the world to run away from God? Take a quick spiritual life check: How's your prayer life? When was the last time you picked up your Bible in private? Score zero? Then you're headed in the wrong direction—you need to get down on your knees before you walk out that door to freedom (and if you go on out slamming the door behind you, my theory will be proof-tested!).

All those checks safely passed, you are ready to go through the door. The question is: to what? Those dreams we've been talking about? Maybe now is the time. No matter that you're not prepared—go back to school and get prepared. Sure, it costs money but look at it as an insurance policy—if your husband gets so anxious for heaven that he goes first, you can support yourself! Goodness knows, you can't live on the widow's mite in this day of inflation.

So head out for your nearest trade school or college and talk to a counselor. Don't worry about being older than the rest of the students. In the first place there will be some older than you, and second, you have had a lifetime of experience that will add to every exam you write. Most professors have gotten over the threat of the mature woman in the classroom—unless, of course, she assumes that she knows more than he does . . . and says so. That could give you trouble. You just have to learn mouth control because you are simply another student now, not the minister's wife whom everyone turned to for answers. You wanted freedom from the parsonage? You've got it, complete without rank and privileges. Maybe you never realized that you were somebody special before or you always wished people would *not* put you in a special place in their minds. Wish granted! Nothing like school to make you understand the freedom the rest of the people in the world have. Pass or fail, that's it! Freedom to make it on your own.

You say it was a paycheck you had in mind? Great! Dishwashers earn $1.85 an hour if they're lucky. Well, you didn't expect to start at the top, did you? Being a waitress doesn't fit the life-style you're used to? And besides, people in the church would talk? You had in mind something more—like being a secretary or receptionist. How's your shorthand—or for that matter, your longhand? You have your teaching credentials? Great, if they're current. But maybe you'd better test out the classroom situation today by substituting and see if you can stand the pressure. Teachers don't get the same respect they did when you were in school. Better find out if you can hack it. In fact, are you sure you can work eight hours a day, five days a week? Forty hours of freedom a week can surely make you tired!

The fact is that you may be a whiz at women's society (or in the bedroom), but you may be the most inexperienced person in the land when it comes to employment! If this thought threatens you, reassure yourself that you are thinking young—like a teen-ager, in fact, who can't get a job without experience and can't get experience without a job! Instant empathy! Actually, you probably have some experience valuable to an employer—you just have to recognize it. How many bulletins have you typed? Did you keep those account books for nothing? You set up the church office filing system? Good. That's business experience. A lifetime of meeting and dealing with people should surely count in applying for a receptionist job. Do you speak and write well? Maybe public relations for a small firm is the place to start. What about all those years teaching little children in church school—could it possibly qualify you for a teacher's aid position or nursery school? You're an excellent seamstress? Then show your ability to the fabric shop and hire on as a teacher. Likewise with handicrafts. Maybe you are terrific at organizing—then take a look at YWCA programs, community senior citizens' projects. You have had more experience than most; you just have to convince the employer that you can do what you say you have done. But say it—on the application form, in the interview, wherever you are asked for such information. Don't be ashamed of your cloistered life—it could give you "cloistrophobia" . . .

So now you're free to brag a little about what you've been doing these last ten years or so. Even if you never get a job, your ego will have had a boost just discovering that you have been doing *something*. The spinning-my-wheels syndrome will begin to diminish slightly, and you'll begin to realize you are a valuable person—sort of. Unless, of course, you really haven't done a darn thing but sit in the back row, trying to stay as uninvolved as possible. Ironically, if that's the case, you may have to volunteer your services for awhile to prove your worth. United Crusade, the Red Cross, government programs are constantly looking for helpers (who, incidentally, help themselves). Your denomination may even use your services at an area level, and that may be the thing you really are experienced in! Free to serve a new way—what a nifty freedom!

Meantime back at the manse . . .

Strange things may be happening to your husband. Action begets reaction, and your husband may face the fact that his Garden Outside Eden is beginning to look like a weed patch. He comes home for lunch and has to open a can of soup (same food as before, only *you* opened the can!). An urgent call home for you to run an errand is made before he realizes that you aren't there to do his bidding. He reaches into the closet on Friday, the day before a working gal's washday, only to discover that all his good shirts are gone. That never happened before, but then you never went two weeks without doing the ironing before. The monthly gas bill for the car arrives, and he is startled to discover it has almost doubled. The poor man is bewildered. His life pattern is all out of kilter. Where order existed, there is now disorder. The things you did together he finds himself doing alone because you're gone or too tired to go. In short, he feels deserted.

Mind you, he may have agreed to what you are doing—perhaps even encouraged you. He just had no idea how dependent he had become. You were always there, so it happened naturally. Now when the phone rings in an empty house, it makes his stomach feel funny, and lunch alone isn't very pleasant. You have been his counselor and confidant perhaps. Now your hours are "after six only." Suddenly he feels that he's in this thing alone.

You are not responsible for his feelings except in a side-effect way. (What was just the right prescription for you had side-effects on him.) Actually, your step into a new life-style is causing him to reevaluate his life. It may be the first time he has ever thought seriously about the fact that he—and only he—is in the ministry. He may have assumed all these years that even though you didn't get a paycheck . . . I can't finish that sentence. Surely there is not a minister left among us who expects —yea, demands—full concurrence and obedient co-operation from his spouse. Even God accepts us on a voluntary basis . . .

But change he will, and you must be ready. For example, you may land a very good job indeed, and your first paycheck equals his (with his fifteen years seniority!). That can wipe out a man's ego—even after taxes! He takes a fresh look at what the church considers his very good salary level, acutely aware that in the business world he could be earning twice as much. Now, he always knew this. It's just that this time he sees it—in the form of your paycheck. Perchance he has a reaction opposite to threat, however. He has visions of a Porsche in the garage, a sailboat at the lake by your new cottage, and *you* begin to wonder if the materialism he has preached against was evil only because he didn't have any. Then you discover that his sermons really haven't done you much good either because you had all kinds of plans for the money in your hand and he is standing there spending it for you. Well, whose money do you think you've been spending all these years if not his? So why shouldn't he expect to spend yours?

Back to that first question before you went out the door—how important is your marriage to you? You have the wherewithal to go through the door now and never return if you want. You are self-supporting. Take a good long look at that man of yours and the years behind you. Freedom is going to cost you dearly if you lose him in the rush for a new life. Thus you make a discovery: freedom always has limits that, if cast off, make the very thing we search for the thing that destroys us. Quick—before you weaken—sit down and start planning how to use the money together. That's the road to freedom.

Some other strangely pleasant things may begin to happen to your husband. You may discover him in

157

animated conversation with a friend talking about . . . you of all things. There he sits bragging about the new you, your newly acquired capabilities, the exciting things you're doing. Stay stunned long enough to keep your mouth shut and listen. Discovery of discoveries: he likes what is happening to you!

You become vaguely aware that he is often more attentive, getting up to pour *your* coffee, doing little things around the house that were strictly your jurisdiction before, finding other people to do church jobs he used to let fall naturally on your shoulders. Now that he has discovered you're not in competition with him and don't intend to leave him he reacts with a new security. He's more interesting. In sum, your liberation has liberated him, too—from the need to provide all the living to the pleasant sharing of increased resources . . . from dependence upon you to self-sufficiency . . . from taking you for granted to consideration and mutual respect . . . from seeing you as his wife to seeking you as an exciting person.

If you achieve all that by going through the front door, you have been liberated and then some! The things these pages don't say are the pitfalls of emotional innuendos, subjective feelings, and disillusionments that clutter the landscape in the search for such freedom. No two people begin with the same relationship, and yours may be holier than some (theirs may be whole!). Work may be a drudge, school a failure, and home a welcome refuge. Going out may, in fact, be the only way to discover how much freedom you already have.

Then there is the ever-present church. Somewhere along your search you have to decide what to do with it. As long as your husband is a minister and you are his wife, the church is a part of your lives. You can turn your back on it, take a spite-filled attitude, or accept it as a wholesome part of your being, but you have to do something. Neutrality is rarely the answer. Life in the parsonage will see to that. For the first time you will begin to understand why the women who work say "no" when asked to help. They honestly don't have the time to do more, especially if the family is still at home. The price of your work in the church will be higher now than it has ever been in your life—and therefore, *can* be more meaningful if you choose to let it be. For now you actually must choose whether to serve or not, and decide how much of your precious time you will give away in order to preserve the fellowship of believers in our society. You may not have meant for this to happen, but accidentally the time you contribute to the church now makes you keenly aware of the value of your faith. Before, it was taken—often taken for granted—and now it is given. That is freedom.

Let us not presume naïveté to the point that everyone in your husband's congregation will approve of your newfound freedom. They will not. Men, especially, are prone to threat. What if their wives should follow suit? The faithful workers may feel somehow put upon that the minister's wife is no longer supporting them. If they are not doing their work out of a cheerful heart, you may be the object of criticism. So, beware! The critic speaks because he is dissatisfied with himself, unless you give him room to criticize justly by taking no part at all.

Your husband is also left less protected than before and sometimes gets lonely. You will have to work harder to create sharing times. If communication was important before, it is essential now. So are good times together. Togetherness doesn't just happen any more; it is created —and you with your husband are the creators. Leave this task unattended, and your husband may have more attention than he can handle—from somebody else! Even sex takes a little more effort. Time that was short before is now almost abbreviated out of existence. A nooner becomes a quickie—and Beat the Clock a way of night life. You may even have to be late for work some morning just to maintain something like normalcy . . .

These are the demands of your new freedom. Freedom has limitations, and so do you. Know where those limits are or you could lose your Self while trying desperately to find it. You may discover that you are now mother, wife, employee, minister's wife, and church member. Instead of not having enough to do, you are going under doing too much.

In all things be temperate. Those have got to be the hardest words in the New Testament . . . Work can be important, but overwork can do you in. Women's Lib may have arrived complete with Wonder Woman, but you may not be the artist's model—only the cartoon.

There is a remote possibility that you have merely endured this chapter to see what rantings and ravings would emerge from this mundane sage (at least I'm spicy sometimes!). Don't give up—there's only one chapter to go, and besides, if you are brilliantly happy, totally unaffected by any of the demands of liberated women, then just tear this chapter out and give it to someone you think may be dwelling in a Parsonage Prison—along with a cup of cold water . . . Better yet, save it to read again ten years from now when you're ready.

12
Let this Cup
Pass from Me

"When are you going to get out of the house so we can fix it up for the next man?" The question was thrown out innocently enough, but it caught the minister wrong. He spun on his heels and retorted angrily, "You can have it at three o'clock this afternoon." At 3:00 P.M. the parsonage stood empty.

Fortunately, not many men leave the ministry quite like that, but leave they do, in what sometimes seems like droves—especially if they are your friends. In fact, you rarely stay in without thinking about getting out! Not every day, of course, but three—maybe forty—times in your ministry the question will rear its ugly head. You can stuff it down, but it will pop up again whenever your dissatisfaction level gets high or your feelings get mauled. And you have to answer it every single time because the situations are always different—and so are you.

There are few other jobs in the world so wound into the total structure of a person as the ministry is. Read the histories of great preachers—they read like a page out of parapsychology. Struck down with light . . . a tap on the shoulder . . . hearing your name called in mid-air . . . knowing there is nothing else in the world you can do but preach. The catch is that not all the ministers at work today are great preachers who have been struck by an enlightening bolt. Some have quietly resolved to give the church their life as their way of serving God. Others see the church as the instrument of salvation in society and want to be on the saving end. Some are attracted by the ideological concepts and see the church as the best place to use their minds. And some see it as the way to change men's lives.

But even as it changes the lives of men, it affects the lives of those who serve in it. They are changed for better or for worse—and so are their wives and families. Who they were in the beginning and what their purpose was in entering the church determines to a large degree how they will answer the question of leaving the ministry when it comes to them. In the beginning they stand in their ordination robes, young, full of idealism, sure they will set the church on fire, and innocent as lambs led to the slaughter.

The one thing that no seminary can teach, or for that matter no medical school or law school, is how to cope with the dailiness. There may have been an attempt to give some counseling skills, a lot of teaching about preaching and thinking, some psychology to help you understand people, and maybe some intern programs in which the prospective pastor actually worked in on-the-job training. It's all good—and it's all pretty unreal. (And very little different from any other educational training in that respect!) During seminary a visiting church official asked what we wives did all week while our husbands were off in school. I couldn't resist saying that we stayed home and ran the church while our husbands were off learning how. He laughed, but it was true. I lived at the student charge while my husband went off to school. *Somebody* had to answer the phone, host the midweek study group, tend the emergencies that arose while he was gone. And believe me, it's in the everyday things that the real ministry occurs, not the main event on Sunday morning.

The first thing a man has to learn when he finishes school is how to translate what he has been taught into words and actions that speak to his people—and that's not easy. Is there a seminary so brave as to offer a course in "Coping with the Cantankerous"? Or how about "Ways and Means of Changing Centuries-Old Attitudes"? A mini-course in telephone diplomacy that offers skill in hanging up gracefully might be entitled "For Whom the Bell Tolls." In fact, the course could be expanded to include bell choirs, organ chimes, and steeple bells (it took a week to get ours operating again after my husband got them stuck ringing them too vigorously). Another essential rarely supplied in ministerial training is a course in "Office Practices" which prepares a man to write bulletins, church papers, brochures, and then type, mimeograph, fold, and mail them with speed and efficiency. This could be simplified by a companion course in "Organizing and Managing the Volunteer Worker." The list is unending, but by now you can see that part of the problem is that seminary training doesn't completely tell it like it is—nor could it. Life becomes the teacher and sometimes we have real difficulty learning the lessons, especially if our expectations differ greatly from the reality of every day.

Your man, for example, may have come into the ministry to work with people and has found himself spending so many hours as an administrator that he rarely has time to get to the individual people. There are endless boards and committees, budget meetings and preparations, property to attend to—all important and all time-consuming. It is also possible that he has made the startling discovery that he is the only Indian in a tribe of Chiefs—what everybody dreams up he is expected to carry out. This makes him feel like the Chief Flunky whose greatest talent is moving tables, stacking chairs, replacing light bulbs, and locking up. Instead of being pastor, counselor, and preacher he is office manager, clerk typist, and janitor (with PBX thrown in for good measure). To say the least, it isn't quite what he had in mind . . .

Once the reality is established he must then struggle with the fact that it might last forever. Thus begins the Greener Pastures Syndrome. He fully knows that it is not possible for one man to do all the things expected of him—and they are expected—so he concludes that if he works very hard his achievements will be recognized so that he can move to a larger church where more than one minister is on the staff. That way some of the responsibility can be designated to the other man and, of course, to the janitor and church secretary. This twists his original motivation for entering the ministry slightly but is justified since the end result is to get back to the original motivation. He struggles for three or four years and receives his second assignment and his second confrontation with reality.

True, he is promoted (if increased salary and membership equal promotion) but not nearly the way he thought he might be. He looks around and discovers other men jumped to much larger parishes than his, and suddenly be becomes victimized by self-doubt. What has he done wrong? Perhaps his work has the wrong emphasis? Or maybe the other fellows are playing politics—

maybe they have an "in"! Then comes the biggest jolt of all—in the larger church nothing much is different. True, there is a part-time secretary and a janitor who cleans once a week, but the problems are the same—only more so. There are *more* people demanding his time, more people wanting him to perform in their prescribed manner, more critics, more counseling, more committees—and he must still fight to find time to prepare a sermon or plan a worship service. He is running harder just to keep up. There is less time to spend with his growing family, more demands on his meager income; and suddenly looms the question: Should I get out? Maybe I'm not really suited to the ministry . . .

And sometimes he isn't—or you aren't. As he has struggled with the realities of the pastorate, you, his wife, are constantly affected by them also. It may be the shortness in his voice after a long day, or the loneliness as you sit home with the children night after night, the distance that creeps in between you because you simply don't have time to nurture your marriage. You may even be asking your own questions: Have I made a mistake? Am I really cut out to be the wife of a minister? Your perspective has gradually changed, since everywhere you turn you are introduced as the wife of the minister until you have begun to think of yourself as the minister's wife instead of the wife of the man you fell in love with.

It is possible that he is coping well and you are losing the game. You may have been meant to live a quiet, retiring life, and instead you find yourself always being forced into activity. Perhaps you never prayed a public prayer in your life, only to discover that it is now a frequent request. You may be so shy that meeting people is sheer agony, and yet you must constantly mix with strangers. It is of little help if your husband is well liked and much in demand as a speaker, for it only increases your inner struggle.

While you were in seminary, you and your husband may have spent many happy hours together, going places, visiting friends, attending programs, and now you find yourself constantly separated. You go alone to women's meetings, you sit alone in church (beside someone, but alone), you take communion alone. There is no money for sitters, so you spend many evenings by yourself; and when your husband has a free evening, there is no money to go to a special place. In fact, he probably is so glad to be at home that to ask him to go out would be an insult.

As your children begin to grow, you make your own disturbing discovery. *You* are raising the children. He may actually see them more than other fathers see their children, but his time comes in bits and pieces and you are the one who must weave the tapestry of their lives. Even if he tries very hard to overcome the pull of his work so that there is time for the family, you begin to realize that it is rare for his mind, as well as his body, to be completely present. The seminary never told you about this—if it told *you* anything at all . . .

So what do you do when your husband pops the question? "Should we leave the ministry?" may come to you as the dawn of a new day, a chance for a more peaceful, normal life. Perhaps now you see an end to moving, to the constant struggle of making home out of houses that are never permanent, never yours. Here is your chance to put down roots so your children are not shuffled from school to school, from friendships to friendships. Your state of mind when the question comes to him may be the deciding factor. It could even be the reason he asked the question. Think long before you answer. If you are the only one who wants to leave, will he truly be happy doing some other kind of work? Does he actually want to leave, or is he just toying with the idea because he is in a tough spot? This answer should take awhile.

And so some decide that this way of working with people really isn't what they wanted to do. They feel their real ministry is such a meager part of their life that they are in fact denying it. In addition, their lifestyle is causing suffering and hardship to the family unit, stifling the kind of marriage and home life they desire. So they step out into a new way of working with people that better suits them.

Others decide to stay with it a while longer, to make a renewed effort to face themselves and their dreams for both the ministry and the family. The search for an answer has helped them understand themselves better and drawn them closer together. They plunge back into the work with renewed vigor and determination. Somehow, they also become a little more accepting of the seeming inequities of the church and their life pattern. They settle in for the long haul.

Then something happens they never expected. It comes on slowly and grows into a many-faceted thing. A cause, an interest, a specific idea becomes the focal point of their ministry. More and more time is spent implementing programs, writing about ideas, putting concepts into action. Eventually, their involvement with this interest grows until it comes into conflict with the other demands of pastoral work. A different kind of decision has to be made, for if this happens to a man, he finds himself a specialist in a field of generalists. He never intended this to occur, it just did. And now he is irritated by having to leave his consuming interest to go to finance meetings or speak at fellowship suppers. He would rather—and does—fly off to Washington to meet with the person who can help him effect the change he sees possible. He spends time writing about his subject to convince others of its importance. Counseling becomes an interruption, preaching a hardship (except when he talks about *his* subject), and the quibbling over church affairs suddenly seems petty and unimportant. Your man is ready to catapult out of the church. When the right offer comes, he will jump at it so fast as to make your head spin. The decision to leave will be a decision to go—and rightly so. He can accomplish more by zeroing in on his interest than he ever would while making a halfhearted attempt at carrying on a ministry.

Speaking of offers, one of the most tempting forms of exiting the ministry is the route of the Great Job Offer. Aside from the salary, which is almost always considerably more than your present one, the offer holds the lure of nine to five, weekends off, paid vacations without guilt (or frequent calls to see how things are going), and unlimited promotions. These offers can often be in related fields that present an alternate type of ministry in such things as probation work, drug abuse centers, private counseling. It is easier—and more natural—to go into a related field since the man is continuing his original motivation of working with people in a helping capacity. Much more difficult is the opportunity that holds strictly secular employment for money's sake. To accept such an offer would, for some, be a rejection of the several years of life they have invested in the ministry. Unless he is in total rebellion against the church and God or was completely miscast at the start, the minister is more likely to be comfortable using words working among and with many people, and being permitted self-expression.

How the job offer is received is often determined by moods of mind or conditions of life described here as separate reasons for leaving the ministry. The man—your man—may have been living with the question of leaving for a long time but he has submerged it so that he can do his work. Nothing dramatic enough has happened to make the question a vital issue, but he may feel a deep-seated discontent that is seldom put into words. When the offer comes, it has particular appeal because the minister's inner condition makes him receptive. At least five excellent job offers have come my husband's way, and each time they have come when he was facing crisis in his own life—either in the church we were serving or in his Self. Searching through these offers has helped us to understand why we stay, but has also helped us realize why others leave. These jobs have offered us wealth, status, and even fame, but they would not be the totalness of ministry the church represents. The job offer, like no other reason for leaving the ministry, makes you discover what you like about what you are doing!

Another insidious form of gnawing that can drain the life out of your husband's ministry is disillusionment with the system, the organizational structure of the church and its politics. The key word to understanding is organization. The church is not the message; it is the vehicle. Somehow we think that it should be free from men jostling for position on important boards, struggling to be known and seen at conferences and conventions.

Jealousies and resentments over other men's promotions and our own just should not occur between men who are there to preach the gospel of love. And that's right —they shouldn't . . . but they do. Because even as people have expectations for us as ministers' wives that we do not hold for ourselves, ministers have personal expectations for their lives that we may not comprehend. And they are human in the way they go about achieving those expectations.

Unfortunately, the individual man—your husband— may feel that the system is so big he doesn't count. Then when no one seems to care about the work he is doing, when other men are all so busy that there is very little fellowship with his co-workers, or when he is sent to a town in a desolate valley, far removed from any other churches or ministers of his denomination, he may feel very lonely indeed. (Some men feel just the opposite— relieved finally to be left alone to do their ministry the way they want to!) Then, as time after time the system fails to reward him for work well done, either by the assignments he receives or by failing to make him a responsible part of the larger church, the desolation consumes him and he exits quietly, believing that he wasn't really wanted. He leaves, hating the church for what it has done to him, full of disillusionment and contempt.

Somewhere along the line someone, maybe you, should have pointed out that we're all in the system together. It doesn't make or break us—we do it to ourselves. The system isn't perfect any more than the men who established it, but the way to change it is to stay in and work at the change. The man outside the gate no longer holds the key to unlock the door so that fresh ideas can blow through the church. That happens from the inside. But you have to believe it can happen, and you must have a firm grip on who you are and how important you really are—or are not. Sometimes the church is blamed when the man needs to change, but no one has helped him to see this so he continues "hit and miss" through life, trying to discover what his niche should be.

There must be as many reasons for leaving the ministry as there are men who have left, but the one that looms above all else is the disintegration of the family unit. Some marriages just aren't made in heaven and can't make it on earth. They never should have happened in the first place. Add the pressures of the ministry to an unsteady marriage, and it caves in. Remember, though, it probably would have caved in no matter what the job. But the question remains, awaiting an answer: Did the life imposed upon the family by the ministry cause it to come apart? Inevitably the answer must sometimes come back "yes."

For all the ridiculous remarks on these pages, the life of a minister *is* unique, its demands upon his family are sometimes heavy, and the emotions are sometimes stretched taut. It does demand a discipline in living that enables you to work harder, teaches you to enjoy the simple blessings of love and good fellowship, requires you to be astute with finances, and encourages you to be open to everyone around you. It forces you either to draw closer together or to be pulled apart. But in this life-style, *as in any other*, we must each make our daily choices that finally compound into the life we live. Each of us must decide the kind of person we will be and the God relationship we will allow—and give every other person the freedom to make the same choices. Leaving the ministry is one of those choices.

171

Sixteen years ago my husband stood for ordination with a class of twenty-nine men. Today only eleven of those men remain in the pastoral ministry. None of us know if a year from now—or ten—we will be different persons from what we are today, and the question may be ours to answer. Whether we leave or stay will depend on who we have become with each passing day. Five times we have chosen to stay, but we are aware that, like many of our friends, we may someday be led to take the step they have.

Meantime, we continue to be nourished by the joys of this way of life. There is no other occupation that allows you such complete sharing in the life events of so many people as does this one. To consecrate the tiny infant of a young couple you married, to lead a family teetering on the edge of disintegration back to wholeness, to hold the hand of the sufferer, to bring hope to the despairing by finding them a job or a home, to stand by the bereaved—these are the privileges of the ministry. And to be surrounded by loving people who search for faith as they practice it, who know how to laugh from their souls, who pray for you and support you when you are in need—these are the joys of the ministry. Always to have a home to move to, to have people who care enough to lend a hand, to feel the pull of fellowship in worship that strengthens and renews—these, too, are joys of the ministry. No words can describe the surge of love that can grow between you and your congregation, the friends who remain close all your life, the privilege of knowing and working closely with thousands of people in a lifetime. These, too, are the joys of the ministry.

And above all, there is the supreme joy of seeing a

person become a changed creature because he has come face to face with his Lord, Jesus Christ. For this *is* the ministry!

To stand beside a noble man who loves God and his people, who struggles with his own capabilities—or lack of them—who thinks little of his life but to give it away . . . such is a life not accorded to many. To live it with joy there is but one key: be open to yourself, to others, and to God. Love will then be your companion, and being a minister's wife not so bad. In fact, I hope that after awhile you might think it's pretty terrific!

Because it is . . .

The Last Word

Here is your chance to contribute to a worthy cause. Tear out 10 percent of this book, whatever strikes your fancy, and give it to a friend you think should read it. *Then* recommend the book. That way more people will buy the book—and, of course, you will have to buy another copy because yours is now damaged. And you can write your purchase out of tithe since all the proceeds earned are dedicated to assisting a particular Samoan congregation build their dream. An instant "Reading for Missions" project for your whole church! Your neighborhood! Your city! So tithe your book now, before you forget . . .

And I hope that someday you are lucky enough to meet so beautiful a person as Dorothy Wilson, who patiently endured these pages to produce a masterpiece of typing! The Presbyterian Church is fortunate to have such a lay person, and this Methodist minister's wife is blessed to have such a friend. May you be so blessed when you write your own book.